Western Tradition and Naturalistic Hindi Theatre

ASIAN
THOUGHT
AND
CULTURE

Sandra A. Wawrytko
General Editor

Vol. 58

PETER LANG
New York • Washington, D.C./Baltimore • Bern
Frankfurt am Main • Berlin • Brussels • Vienna • Oxford

Diana Dimitrova

Western Tradition and Naturalistic Hindi Theatre

PETER LANG
New York • Washington, D.C./Baltimore • Bern
Frankfurt am Main • Berlin • Brussels • Vienna • Oxford

Library of Congress Cataloging-in-Publication Data

Dimitrova, Diana G.
Western tradition and naturalistic Hindi theatre / Diana Dimitrova.
p. cm. — (Asian thought and culture; v. 58)
Includes bibliographical references and index.
1. Hindi drama—20th century—History and criticism.
2. Ashk, Upendra Nath, 1910– —Literary style. 3. Hindi drama—
Western Influences. I. Title. II. Series.
PK2041.D56 891.4'3271—dc21 2003054583
ISBN 0-8204-6822-3
ISSN 0893-6870

Bibliographic information published by **Die Deutsche Bibliothek.**
Die Deutsche Bibliothek lists this publication in the "Deutsche Nationalbibliografie"; detailed bibliographic data is available on the Internet at http://dnb.ddb.de/.

The paper in this book meets the guidelines for permanence and durability of the Committee on Production Guidelines for Book Longevity of the Council of Library Resources.

275 Seventh Avenue, 28th Floor, New York, NY 10001
www.peterlangusa.com

Printed in Germany

На мама и татко

Table of Contents

Part Two

Western Tradition and Upendranāth Aśk 's Dramatic Style

A Note on Transliteration and Translation

The system of transliteration in this work follows a standard system for Hindi, in which long vowels are marked with a macron, for instance *ā*, retroflex consonants with a dot beneath the letter, for example *ḍ*. Nasalization is indicated by the sign *ṃ* which follows the nasalized vocal, for instance *gāṃv* and *kahāniyāṃ*. No special symbol is used for *anusvāra* in the transliteration, the appropriate nasal consonant being written to avoid confusion in the pronunciation, for example *ekāṅkī* and *raṅgmañc*. All Hindi names are spelled according to the transliteration system for Hindi, for example *Aśk*. The names of languages, cities and countries that have common Roman spellings have not been marked with diacritics, thus *Hindi* and not *Hindī*, *Delhi* and not *Dillī*.

All translations from Hindi into English in this book are my own.

Introduction

Hindi Drama and the Naturalist Upendranāth Aśk

Two main tendencies mark the development of Hindi drama. The dramatists who can be associated with the first tendency follow in the steps of Jayśaṅkar Prasād (1889–1937). His plays deal with historical subject matter and are written in a rather artificial and elevated Sanskritized Hindi. Their numerous scenes and acts and the personages' long monologues, which are in conformity with the aesthetic of Sanskrit drama, make it difficult to present his plays on stage.

The representatives of the second school are influenced by the social problem plays of naturalists Ibsen and Strindberg. In using topical subject matter, everyday language and new dramatic techniques, for which most authors are indebted to Western drama, the playwrights aim at reaching a broad audience in a theatre. Thus, it becomes important to write plays in conformity with the requirements of the stage. Major playwrights are Lakṣmīnārāyaṇ Miśra (b. 1903), Bhuvaneśvar (1912–1957), Jagdīścandra Māthur (1917–1981), Mohan Rākeś (1925–1972) and Upendranāth Aśk (1910–1996).

Upendranāth Aśk's dramatic production spans several decades before and after India's Independence. His work manisfests a creative encounter with Western naturalism and was received positively in the 1940s and 1950s. In the 1960, the period of the nationalization of Indian theatre, dramatists were required to emancipate themselves from Western dramatic influence and begin writing in the mode of either classical Sanskrit drama or Indian folk theatre. This shift in ideology led to a negative reception of Aśk's naturalistic dramatic production after the 1960s. The comprehensiveness and controversial reception of Aśk's dramatic oeuvre have prompted me to choose this playwright as a focus of research in this book.

The literary legacy of Upendranāth Aśk (1910-1996) comprises many novels and numerous anthologies of plays, short stories, poems, and works of literary criticism. The author is the first Indian playwright who was awarded the National Sangeet Natak Akademi Prize in 1956, and was thus acknowledged as the foremost dramatist of Hindi. In 1972 he received the Soviet Land Nehru Award for the totality of his literary production.

Despite all the awards and the comprehensiveness of his oeuvre, Aśk has been studied very little by Hindi literary critics. Two monographs on his most famous novel *Girtī Dīvāreṃ* (*Falling Walls*), 1947, appeared several decades after its publication [Gaeffke 1966, 1978; Shonek, n.d.]. The revised shortened version of this novel, Hindi title *Cetan (Cetan)*, 1952, was translated into Russian in 1961.[1] A dissertation that studies Aśk's much disputed place in Hindi literature on the material of the *Girtī Dīvāreṃ* series was published in 1998.[2]

The Western reader is acquainted with Aśk's most representative short stories through their English, German and Russian translations.[3] However, Aśk's dramatic work is still unknown to the Western world. Georg Buddruss has pointed to the fact that the former Soviet Union remains the only Western country where research on Aśk's plays has been done [Buddruss 1976, 1981].[4] One cannot fail to notice the scarcity of critical

---

[1] Upendranath Aśk, *Padajuščie steny* (Moskva: Izdatel'stvo inostrannoj literatury, 1961).

[2] A.D. Rockwell, *The Novelty of Ashk: Conflict, Originality and Novelization in the Life and Work of Upendranath Ashk*, diss., U of Chicago, 1998 (Ann Arbor: UMI, 1998) 9832167.

[3] U. Ashk, "The Dark Saahabs," *Indian Literature* 23/3 & 4 (1980): 249-57; ——, "Winter," *Indian Literature* 17/3 (1974): 129-30; ——, "In the Asylum," *Journal of South Asian Literature* 19/1 (1984): 111-16; ——, "Mr. Ghatpande," *Journal of South Asian Literature* 19/1 (1984): 101-9; ——, "The Marsh," *Hindi Review* 5/6 (1960): 221-5; ——, "The Oil-Man of Kakrhan," *Hindi Review* 1/7 (1956): 22-36; ——, "The Rickshaw-Puller," *Hindi Review* 2/3 (1957): 93-101; *Der sprechende Pflug. Indien in Erzaehlungen seiner besten zeitgenoessischen Autoren*, ed. W.A. Oerley (Herrenalb, Schwarzwald: Erdmann, 1962); *Der Tigerkoenig. Erzaehlungen und Kurzgeschichten aus Indien* (Berlin: Volk und Welt, 1973); U. Aśk, *Pustynja: Rasskazy* (Leningrad: Chudojestvennaja literatura, 1973).

[4] The following studies should be mentioned: S. Potabenko, "K istorii razvitija sceničeskoj dramaturgii i teatra chindustani," *Literatury Indii. Sbornik statej*, ed. I.S. Rabinovič i E.P. Celyśev (Moskva: Izdatel'stvo vostočnoj literatury, 1958) 105-148; S.I. Potabenko, *Dramaturgija chindi v bor'be za svobodu i nezavisimost' Indii* (Moskva: Izdatel'stvo

studies on Aśk's dramas in India as well.[5] Most of the literature consulted for this volume contains only superficial references to Aśk. Though he is generally acknowledged to be one of the most prominent Hindi playwrights, few critics illustrate their theories using his plays as examples. It would not be exaggerated to claim that research on Aśk's dramatic work is a desideratum in the field of study of modern Hindi literature and South Asian cultural studies.

Aśk's literary biography was influenced by the socio-cultural climate and historical events of his time. The dramatist's social background, the influence of Indian progressivism and of Western naturalistic theatre accounted for his realistic and socially committed mode of writing. Aśk was affiliated closely with both the Indian Progressive Writers' Association and the Indian People's Theatre Association, and the Parimal society, which was opposed to the dogmatism of the progressivist movement. The purposefulness and social commitment of the playwright's work bears witness to the progressivist message of his dramatic oeuvre. Thus, the author exposes social evils of Indian society and points to women's oppression. He criticizes existing social conditions in order to promote reforms. The peculiarities of his literary style, marked by experimentalism and innovative techniques, an open-ended quality and a distanced tone, have

---

vostočnoj literatury, 1962); S. Rabinovič, "P'esa 'Puti raschodjatsja' kak važnejśij etap stanovlenija realizma v tvorčestve Upendranatha Aśka, " *Dramaturgija i teatr Indii, sbornik statej* (Moskva: Izdatel'stvo vostočnoj literatury, 1961) 189-234; N.A. Viśnevskaja, *Indijskaja odnoaktnaja drama* (Moskva: Izdatel'stvo Nauka, 1964). Aśk's one act plays *Pardā uṭhāo, pardā girāo* and *Lakṣmī kā svāgat* are translated by Viśnevskaja and are included in the last chapter of her book. A Russian translation of the play *Alag alag rāste* is also available: U. Aśk, *Puti razchodjatsja: p'esa v treh dejstvijah*, trans. I. Kudrevceva and I. Rabinovič (Moskva: Izdatel'stvo inostrannoj literatury, 1957); There is an unpublished M.A. thesis, which studies twelve one act plays by Aśk. See K. Zwecker, "Interpretation zwoelf ausgewaehlter Einakter von Upendranath Ashk," M.A. thesis, Johannes Gutenberg Universitaet zu Mainz, 1980. Two years ago I published my doctoral thesis on Aśk. See D. Dimitrova, *Upendranāth Aśk's Dramatic Work: Women and Gender in Modern Hindi Drama and as Revealed in the Plays of Upendranāth Aśk (1910-1996)*, diss. (Heidelberg: Microfiche Edition, 2000).

[5] Jagadiścandra Māthur, *Nāṭakkār Aśk* (Allahabad: Nīlābh, 1954); U. Siṃh, *Samasyā nāṭakkār Aśk* (Vārāṇasī: Sañjay Buk Senṭar, 1982). There is a chapter on Aśk as a playwright in N. Hemant, *Ādhunik hindī nāṭyakāroṃ ke nāṭyasiddhānt* (Dillī: Akṣar, 1973).

prompted many of Aśk's contemporaries to overlook the progressivist ideal that underlies his literary production.

Though this complexity of literary style accounts for the negative reception by Indian criticism to some extent, the main reasons for his exclusion from the canon of modern Hindi drama are ideological. This book studies Aśk's plays against the background of modern Hindi drama. It deals with the power structures of contemporary critical discourse and makes clear that the issues of Western dramatic influence[6] and ideology[7] account for the exclusion of Aśk from the literary canon of Hindi.

Aśk is influenced by Western dramatic tradition and we can draw parallels between his work and Western drama. He writes realistic plays about social problems in the style of naturalists Ibsen and Strindberg. Similar to them, he explores the problems connected with women's emancipation and relationships between the sexes. However, this influence does not manifest itself in direct borrowing or copying from Western models. Rather, it informs the literary tradition to which Aśk belongs, the atmosphere in which he creates his works and which stimulates his artistic quest. The author sets his plays against the background of contemporary Indian society. His dramatic work can be considered a link, a bridge between Western and Hindi drama. Western influence in Aśk's oeuvre pertains to two aspects, interpretation of women's issues and dramatic style.

---

[6] A detailed study of Aśk's literary biography presupposes an extensive examination of the literary influences the author has experienced in the light of the ideas and method of new historicist criticism. The subject matter and scope of this book will not allow me to deal with the question of literary influence in a comprehensive way. This issue can be the subject of a later monograph on Aśk. See W. Morris, *Toward a New Historicism* (Princeton: Princeton UP, 1972); H. Veeser, *The New Historicism* (New York: Routledge, Chapman & Hall, 1989).

[7] As James Kavanagh points out in his essay on ideology, the term should not be understood narrowly, that is, as it is used in the mass media. "Ideology designates a rich 'system of representations,' worked up in specific material practices, which helps form individuals into social subjects who 'freely' internalize an appropriate picture of their social world and their place in it. Ideology offers the social subject, not a set of narrowly 'political' ideas, but a fundamental framework of assumptions that defines the parameters of the real and the self. " See James H. Kavanagh, "Ideology," *Critical Terms for Literary Study*, ed. Frank Lentricchia and Thomas McLaughlin (Chicago: U of Chicago P, 1990) 310.

As I have already discussed the issues of gender elsewhere, I will focus on the issues of dramaturgy in this book.[8]

The study of Aśk's dramatic method reveals the influence of Western naturalistic dramaturgy and epic theatre on the author. With his dramatic production, Aśk follows the tradition set by his forerunners Miśra and Bhuvaneśvar, and contributes further to the establishment of naturalistic dramaturgy in modern Hindi drama. The author experiments with new forms of figure conception and characterization, and new techniques of presentation of story, plot, time and space. In this way, he enriches the dramatic tradition of modern Hindi.

The playwright employs naturalistic characterization techniques. Thus, his dramatis personae are individuals who are determined by their social milieu. In order to state all the circumstances that have played a role in the formation of the protagonist's character, the author provides as much background information and physical, behavioral and biographical details as possible. Usually, this information is transmitted in the secondary text or narratively, in the figures' speeches, in the form of exposition to the dramas.

The treatment of story and plot points once again to the influence of Western dramaturgy. The main plot in Aśk's dramas is complicated by additional subplots and the action sequences are often coordinated on different fictional levels. In the dramas *Pardā uṭhāo! Pardā girāo* (*Raise the Curtain! Drop the Curtain*) and *Chaṭhā beṭā* (*The Sixth Son)*, the author is one of the first Hindi playwrights to experiment with the insertion of a dream inset or a metaplay into the primary dramatic level. This approach has been inspired by Arthur Miller's and Thornton Wilder's dramaturgy. He is also the first Hindi playwright to introduce the coordination technique of the central self as a device to link the different subplots in the play *Bhaṃvar* (*Whirlpool*).

The influence of Western drama, and especially that of Thornton Wilder, on Aśk is also to be seen in the presentation of time and space. It is characteristic of Aśk's method that he employs mixed forms of time-space structures. Time and space are defined with epic thoroughness. This points to the fact that they serve both to create the illusion of reality on stage and to

[8] See the forthcoming publication D. Dimitrova, *Gender, Religion and Modern Hindi Drama* (forthcoming).

give detailed characteristics of the characters and the circumstances which they have to handle.

Aśk innovates and enriches Hindi theatrical tradition through a creative encounter with Western naturalism. It is the inference of this study that Aśk has been excluded from the literary canon of Hindi on the grounds of ideology. His dramatic style has been influenced by Western theatrical tradition, and not by the poetics of classical Sanskrit or Indian folk theatre. This was antithetical to the new postcolonial definition of the Indian character of Hindi drama during the nationalization of Indian theatre and culture in the 1960s.

On Method

This book is a critical study of Aśk's dramas as literary texts. The scope of this monograph does not allow me to look into the history of reception of the plays. I will deal with modern Hindi drama from its beginnings in the second half of the 19th century until the 1960s. This is the period, during which urban Hindi (proscenium) theatre that originated under Western influence matured and thrived. After the 1960s, dramatists were encouraged to write in the mode of Indian folk theatre. Indian criticism refers to this literary movement as *deśīvād*, nativism. As these dramas originated after the 1960s and were not influenced by Western dramatic tradition, they will not be examined in this book.

Methodologically, two perspectives can be defined in the course of this study. The first one refers to the textual study and thematic analysis of selected plays by six representative dramatists. This gives us an overview of the landscape of the dramatic genre of Hindi from its origination until the 1960s. The second perspective pertains to the critical examination of the dramatic work of one representative author, Upendranāth Aśk. A study of his life, literary biography, and the subject matter of his plays precede the structuralist analysis of his dramaturgical technique and dramatic style.

The study of the historical and socio-cultural background, in which modern Hindi theatre and drama developed, accounts for the emphasis placed on the major literary movements of the 1930s and 1940s on the literary scene of Hindi when discussing the author Aśk. In my view, a cultural and literary study should not deal with a text in isolation from its historical context. It should also consider the historical and cultural circumstances of the production of a literary work. I interpret the dramas not as trans-historical texts, but as deeply rooted in the socio-cultural reality of contemporary Indian society. The issues of dramaturgical technique and dramatic style require a special focus on the formal features of the texts. As I consider Aśk's work most representative of the pre- and post-Independence periods, I base my analysis on his dramatic production.

A close reading of Aśk's dramas as self-sufficient verbal texts seems most appropriate for studying the special case of dramaturgical technique and dramatic style. The semiotic analysis of the author's dramatic production, which interprets the dramatic text as a complex verbal, visual and acoustic super sign activating various socio-cultural codes, accounts for the structuralist method I adopt when discussing the question of dramaturgical technique and dramatic style.

Although structuralist criticism has become very popular in the 1990s and has been applied successfully to the genre of lyrical and narrative texts, it has not dealt with drama yet. In his book on drama criticism, Manfred Pfister points to the "structuralist deficit" in the study of drama, a literary genre that has also been neglected by Russian formalism.[9] The second part of this book aims at presenting a comprehensive structuralist study of Aśk's dramatic work. Special attention is given to instances of Western dramatic influence and the way in which the author reworks Western models in his plays.

---

[9] Pfister states the following two reasons for the absence of structuralist studies on drama. Firstly, drama is a genre whose expressive qualities are not entirely verbal. As Russian formalism was preoccupied with language theory, dramatic texts did not offer easy material to support scholars' ideas. Secondly, the separation of drama research into literary studies and theatre studies has also played a negative role. See M. Pfister, *Das Drama. Theorie und Analyse* (Muenchen: Wilhelm Fink Verlag, 1988) 19. On structuralism, see J. Culler, *Structuralist Poetics: Structuralism, Linguistics and the Study of Literature* (London: Routledge & Kegan Paul, 1975); T. Hawkes, *Structuralism and Semiotics* (London: Routledge, 1988); P. Caws, *Structuralism: The Art of the Intelligible* (Atlantic Highlands, N.J.: Humanities Press International, 1991); J. Lechte, *Fifty Key Contemporary Thinkers from Structuralism to Postmodernity* (London: Routlledge, 1994); P. Pettit, *The Concept of Structuralism: A Critical Analysis* (Berkeley: U of California P, 1977).

Part One

The Playwrights

Chapter One

Neo-Sanskritic and Naturalistic Hindi Drama

General Overview and Periodization

Indian literary criticism refers to the initial three periods of modern Hindi drama up to Independence in 1947 as 'Bhāratendu-kāl' ("Bhāratendu's epoch"), 'Prasād-kāl' ("Prasād's epoch") and 'Prasādottar-kāl' ("post/after-Prasād period"), respectively. In doing so, it alludes to the two major Hindi playwrights of the time whose work is most representative of the development of modern Hindi drama. This periodization follows the tradition of the widely accepted classification of modern Hindi literature that conforms to the lifetime and work of the most prolific and influential authors of Hindi. Thus, we talk about 'Bhāratendu yug', 'Dvivedī yug'[1] and so on.

The 'Prasādottar-kāl', which starts in the 1930s, is followed by the 'svātantryottar-kāl' ("post/after-Independence period") that begins in 1947. This period, in turn, is followed by the 'sāṭhottar-kāl' ("after-the-1960s

---

[1] R.L. Handa even talks of the 'dramas of the Dwivedi era' when referring to L. Miśra's plays, which chronologically belong to the time span immediately after Prasād's period. See R.L. Handa, *History of Hindi Language and Literature* (Bombay: Bharatiya Vidya Bhavan, 1976) 377.

period").[2] Unlike the first three periods in the chronology of modern Hindi drama, which are defined and named after great personalities, the last two time spans in this classification are based on historical events and changes in the political and ideological climate.

Whereas Bhāratendu (1850–1885) heralded the beginning of modern Hindi drama by emancipating it from the conventions of both classical Indian and the commercial Parsi theatre, Prasād (1889–1937) broadened its expressive potential. The power of his language and the depth of psychological characterization of his dramatic figures marked a new phase in the development of modern Hindi drama. While Bhāratendu wrote satirical, lyrical and historical plays, Prasād established the historical play as the main Hindi dramatic genre.

In the 1930s, a generation of playwrights appeared who rebelled against Prasād's authority and the domination of the historical play. They followed in the tradition of Western dramatists Ibsen and Strindberg and wrote not only historical, but also social plays that handled the immediate problems of contemporary Indian society. Their main representative in the 1930s was Lakṣmīnārāyāṇ Miśra (b. 1903).

After Independence, the subject matter of Hindi drama changed. The British were gone; social injustice, however, remained. This prompted many playwrights to stop writing historical plays that glorified the past and saw the British as the only cause for the 'fall' of the great Aryan civilization. The influence of Western drama grew and the social problem play in Hindi thrived. This predominantly social message of modern Hindi drama was in perfect conformity with the ideology of Progressivism, the ideas of Gandhī and Indian National Congress, and the political orientation of the J. Nehrū government toward the Soviet Union and Marxism. The work of Upendranāth Aśk (1910–1996), Jagdīścandra Māthur (1917–1981), Bhuvaneśvar (1912–1957) and Mohan Rākeś (1925–1972) is most representative of this time.

The preoccupation with social issues led in turn to a new 'rebellion' in the 1960s and a new shift in subject matter. The playwrights of the new generation approached the problems of the relationship between man and woman in the family from a more personal perspective. Social issues became less and less topical. In this sense, the plays of Mohan Rākeś,

---

[2] Vacandev Kumār, ed. *Hindī nāṭak: 1960 ke bād* (Paṭnā: Vibhu Prakāṣan, 1982) 12.

Lakṣmīnārāyaṇ Lāl, Hamīdullā and many others should be taken into consideration. Dramaturgically, new techniques were employed. Many Hindi playwrights sought an alternative to the all-pervasive influence of Western drama and took up the folk tradition of the *nauṭaṅkī* as a model of their plays. In this respect, Habīb Tanvīr's and Śāntā Gāndhī's plays should be mentioned.

One could question the universality of this periodization by pointing to the fact that historical plays have been written throughout the entire development of modern Hindi drama and that Western dramatic tradition is as influential nowadays as it used to be in the decades before and after the Independence of 1947. Similarly, Bhuvaneśvar and Upendranāth Aśk placed the emphasis on family issues and the relationship between man and woman from a very personal perspective long before the general shift in this direction in the 1960s.

Though this periodization is not perfect, it reflects the main tendencies and changes in the development of modern Hindi drama objectively. It is current in Indian literary criticism and I will therefore adopt it and will refer to it, wherever necessary, for the purpose of uniformity and clarity.

The Beginnings of Modern Hindi Drama

In the following I will discuss briefly the dramatic work of six representative Hindi playwrights. In this way, we will become acquainted with major Hindi dramatists from the beginnings of modern Hindi theatre until the 1960s. The historical context not only of Aśk's formation as a dramatist, but also of all authors discussed after Prasād draws on Western dramatic tradition. An examination of the works of Aśk's predecessors and contemporaries will provide the historical, cultural and intellectual context for the study of the author's dramatic oeuvre.

Bhāratendu Hariścandra (1850–1885)

The beginning of modern Hindi drama can be traced back to Bhāratendu Hariścandra.[3] To him, drama was the most suitable literary genre for the promotion of his reformatory ideas because of its entertaining potential and power to attract large masses of people, influencing them in an immediate way. That is why he invested all the eighteen plays he wrote with his nationalistic and reformatory views. In order to be more convincing, he rendered them realistic in form, thus deviating from the tradition of the Parsi theatre.

His satirical play *Andher nagarī (The Lawless State),*[4] 1881, exposes the stupidity and absurdity of a society where everything can be bought for one *ṭakā (*"a copper coin, worth half an *anna*"). How does a society that has no values function? The second scene of the play depicts life in a lawless city: a Brahman sells his caste for a *ṭakā*, a Hindu becomes a Muslim for the same amount of money; both cabbage and sweets can be bought for one *ṭakā.*

The ascetic Gobardhan Dās is happy to have found a place where he can get everything so cheap. In scene three, he does not listen to the wise words of his *mahant* ("head priest of a temple") that this is a dangerous city, which he should leave immediately. The following fourth scene is a parody of the "justice" practised by the imbecile king Caupaṭṭ. A subject's goat has died because a door has fallen and has pressed the animal down, causing its death. Trying to find the guilty one, the king questions the carpenter who has provided the wood, the worker who has built the door and so on. Finally

---

[3] For Bhāratendu's formation as a playwright, see V. Dalmia, *The Nationalization of Hindu Traditions: Bhāratendu Hariścandra and Nineteenth century Banaras* (Delhi: Oxford University Press, 1997) 300-14. Dalmia analyses two of Hariścandra's earlier plays, namely *Prem joginī*, (*The Yoginī of Love*), 1874-5, and *Viṣasya viṣamauṣadham*, (*Poison is the Antidote of Poison*), 1876.

[4] Bhāratendu Hariścandra, *Andher nagarī* (Naī Dillī: Śārdā Prakāśan, 1978). In her chapter on Bhāratendu's one act plays, Viśnevskaja translates the title of the play as "Slepoj gorodiško" ("The Blind City"), which is inaccurate. A Hindi equivalent of her Russian translation would have been 'andherī nagarī'. However, this is not the case. 'Andher nagarī' is a fixed expression for 'lawless state.' Cf. N. Viśnevskaja, *Indijskaja odnoaktnaja drama* (Moskva: Nauka, 1964) 31.

the police officer in charge is found guilty for a very absurd reason and has to be hanged as a compensation for the death of the plaintiff's goat. However, the final fifth scene shows the infantry men coming over to the ascetic Gobardhan Dās in order to arrest him and hang him in the place of the police officer.

It turns out that the man who was found guilty happened to be so thin that he did not fit into the loop of the rope, so they had to find somebody who was fat enough for it. The only person who could fit in was the ascetic, so he had to be hanged. The *mahant* manages to save his disciple at the last moment by professing a desire to be hanged in his place. When asked the reason, he explains that the one who is hanged will immediately go to heaven. Thereupon everybody wants to be hanged in the place of the ascetic. The king, who has the supreme authority, reserves this privilege for himself alone and gets hanged.

The dramatist implies that a society that tolerates a lawless state and has no ideals or values is inevitably doomed to fail. Thus, *Andher nagarī* was a powerful and transparent satire of Bhāratendu's time.

In order to communicate his ideas, Bhāratendu had to break with the form of the Sanskrit play. He changed it entirely and created new genres for modern Hindi drama, e.g. the historical, satirical, and lyrical play. His dramaturgical technique and the realistic characterization of the dramatic figures were innovative for modern Hindi drama. They were possible under the influence of the Bengali and English plays, with which Bhāratendu was well acquainted and which he translated into Hindi.

Jayśaṅkar Prasād (1889–1937)

The most prominent representative of the school of the historical drama is Jayśaṅkar Prasād. In his plays, he used historical material in order to draw attention to the present and its problems. At times, his criticism of society is indirect and obscure. It is often intertwined with the author's glorification of the great Hindu past.

I will elaborate on the historical play *Candragupta* (*Candragupta*), 1931,[5] as representative of the twelve plays Prasād wrote on the subject of ancient Indian dynasties. The play, which consists of four acts, is about Candargupta's victory over the Greeks and over the Nanda dynasty in the 4th century B.C. The first act ends with a meeting between Alexander the Great and Candragupta, and the sage Dāṇḍyāyan's prophecy that Candragupta will be the future ruler of India. The second act culminates in Candragupta's victory over the Greeks, led by the army of Seleucus. In the third act the united forces of the states of the Mālvas and the Kṣudrakas manage to overthrow Nanda's rule. Candragupta becomes the new king of Magadha.

The wise Brahman Cāṇakya, who is shown to be the thinker of all complicated political manoeuvres, succeeds not only in bringing together the Mālvas and Kṣudrakas, but also wins the Punjab ruler Parvateśvar for Candragupta's cause. The victory over Nanda and the proclamation of Candragupta as the new ruler of the kingdom of Magadha is shown to be the result of the fight of the united army of the whole of Northern India, and Cāṇakya's skilful management of the political and military situation.

In the last act, the decisive battle with the Greeks, who are led by Alexander's successor, Silyūkas (Seleucus), takes place. Cāṇakya has managed to ensure the support of the Takṣaśilā kingdom as well. The Greeks are defeated and Candragupta consolidates his empire to the West of the river Sindhu. The peace treaty is sealed with a marriage between Candragupta and Karneliyā (Cornelia), Silyūkas's daughter, who is in love with the young emperor and admires the grandeur of India and its culture.

The motif of the superiority of India over Greece is one of the main ideas Prasād communicates to his contemporaries through his play. It is suggested that the nobility, high morality and honesty of its warriors, as illustrated in the characters of Candragupta and the young warrior Siṃharaṇ, is felt and appreciated by the Greeks as well. Talking about her love for India, Karneliyā says that "the other countries are men's birthplaces; India is mankind's birthplace." (*Candragupta*, 127) Even Alexander expresses his admiration for the "soul" of India: "I came to India drawing a sword, having seen a heart, I am going." (*Candragupta*, 130) The marriage between Karneliyā and Candragupta is also to be interpreted symbolically. Prasād

---

[5] Jayśaṅkar Prasād, *Candragupta* (Ilāhābād: Bhārtī Bhaṇḍār, 2017 vi.).

envisaged the interaction between India and Europe or Western civilization as a whole by way of the union of the "body" of Europe and the "soul" of India, as represented by Karneliyā's and Candragupta's characters respectively.[6]

Another motif that underlies the development of the action in the play is the superiority of Hinduism and the Hindu way over Buddhism and Buddhist doctrine. It is no coincidence that Cāṇakya is a Hindu whereas the corrupt Nanda ruler a Buddhist. The injustice and baseness of Nanda's rule and personal moral behavior are opposed to the Brahman's wisdom and nobility. They point to Cāṇakya's superiority. Most of the dramatic figures look up to the Brahman with trust and reverence whenever a difficult and decisive moment comes because of his Brahmanical status. Prasād implies that the glory of India and its heroic past were the result of the people's belief and confidence in Hinduism and Hindu priests. This admiration for traditional Indian learning and wisdom, as reflected in Cāṇakya's figure, is communicated through the opinion of other dramatis personae as well. Thus, Karneliyā talks about her admiration for the *Rāmāyaṇa* and the Brahmans' learning. Even Magadha's Buddhist minister, Rākṣas, who has a rather complicated relation with Candragupta and Cāṇakya throughout the play, acknowledges the Brahman's wisdom and superiority and asks him for forgiveness.

On the other hand, Prasād avoids unrealistic and psychologically untrue pathos in Cāṇakya's portrayal by showing the doubts of some dramatic figures who are closest to him, such as Candragupta. The young prince does not always agree with Cāṇakya's strategy. He does not understand the necessity of cruelty for the sake of a political cause. Thus, Nanda's daughter, Kalyāṇī, who is in love with Candragupta, is exiled together with her father. She kills the Punjab ruler Parvateśvar, who has attempted to abuse her, after he suggests forming a plot against Candragupta. Deserted by everybody and in despair, the young woman commits suicide. Her tragedy is caused by Cāṇakya's deeds. Similarly, Cāṇakya does not hesitate to save Candragupta's life by making Mālvikā sleep in his place in his bed, as he expects plotters to attempt an assault on the prince's life. Mālvikā is

[6] This view reflects the influence of Aurobindo's ideas on the author.

murdered at night. Cāṇakya also drives away Candragupta's parents, as he is afraid that their presence will stand in the way of victory.

All his actions aim at consolidating the whole of India under one ruler, Candragupta. Prasād implies that in the name of the freedom of India, the separate kingdoms should forget their differences and petty quarrels, and unite to fight and win over the alien conqueror, in this case the Greeks. As he puts it in his conversation with the young Āmbhīk, who rules over the Western province of Takṣaśilā and has not joined the union of the other kingdoms yet, Candragupta's kingdom is not the empire of the Magadhas but of the *āryyas* (i.e. "the Indians"). The central message Prasād conveys in *Candragupta* is that his contemporaries should forget their internal conflicts and unite against the British. For the present moment, there could be no higher goal than the independence of India.

In order to communicate his ideas, Prasād refers to Indian history. Though their motifs and characters are moulded in conformity with the author's views, most of the male protagonists like Cāṇakya, Candragupta and Alexander are historical figures. The female characters are, however, entirely fictitious. This gave the playwright the freedom to construct them according to his ideal notion of the feminine.

How are women portrayed in the drama and what are the roles they play?

The main female characters are all positive, capable of self-sacrifice and heroism, and play a crucial role in the events that lead to the victory of India. Prasād suggests that without their active support and collaboration, many of the decisive events would not have been possible. It is interesting to note that Cāṇakya suspects many of the male protagonists of being disloyal or treacherous, but has complete trust in the female characters. The success of many of his actions depends on women's help and reliability, which he never doubts or distrusts.

Thus, Mālvikā sacrifices her life for prince Candragupta. Out of love and care for the young prince, Kalyāṇī kills Parvateśvar, who plots against his life. Similarly, Suvāsinī risks her life and penetrates the camp of the Greeks in order to fulfil Cāṇakya's order and help Rākṣas to find his way back to his own people. Karneliyā does her best to prevent war with the Indians and attempts to instill in her father admiration for Indian culture and convince him that he should not fight the man who has saved her from infamy.[7]

Most interesting is Alkā's character. She plays not only an active social, but also political role in the play. Disgusted by her brother Āmbhīk's greed for power, she leaves her home and goes into exile in the woods, where she meets Candragupta and Cāṇakya and witnesses the sage's prophecy about the young prince's destiny. She is ready to sacrifice her future and marry Parvateśvar, as this is the only way to save the imprisoned Siṃharaṇ whom she loves. It is she, carrying a banner, who leads the people and appeals to them to fight against the Greeks. When Cāṇakya proclaims her and Siṃharaṇ the new rulers of Takṣaśilā, in the place of her brother Āmbhīk, she says that her native kingdom belongs neither to her nor to her brother but to India. It is no coincidence that she saves Cāṇakya's life when Candragupta's insulted father attempts to murder him.

After Cāṇakya and Candragupta, Alkā plays the most significant role in the play. In modern Hindi drama, this is one of the first instances in which so much importance and active political responsibility is attributed to a female character. This is no coincidence, as female characters are central to Prasād's plays. The author portrays women's high morality and readiness for self-sacrifice in the name of their love for their beloved or for their country.

Dramaturgically, Prasād's plays follow in the aesthetic of classical Sanskrit drama. In his article "Raṅgmañc" ("The Stage"), the author points to the fact that modern Hindi drama should not imitate Western theatre. He argues that the West has not achieved the "new" (i.e. Ibsen's plays) by giving up the "old" (i.e. Shakespeare's tradition). Prasād considers Bhāratendu's dramatic work, in which he combines the achievements of both classical Indian and Western theatre, exemplary.[8]

Similarly, in his plays he keeps the tradition of the *dāsīs* ("female slaves") or the main protagonists' companions preceding them on stage and thus introducing their appearance or describing the setting. This explains the large number of dramatis personae in Prasād's dramas. In the play

---

[7] In the first act of the play, Candragupta saves Karneliyā from the Greek Philip, who was going to abuse her.

[8] J. Prasād, "Raṅgmañc," *Kāvya aur kalā tathā anya nibandh*, by J. Prasād (Ilāhābād: Bhārtī Bhaṇḍār, 2015 vi.) 104-6.

Candragupta, their number is thirty. The male figures Devbāl, Nāgdatt and the *gaṇ-mukhya* ("the chief of the community"), and the female servants Nīlā, Līlā and Elis appear on stage only to announce the coming of another personage or to receive an order to deliver a message, etc.

The author preserves another feature of classical Sanskrit drama, namely the beginning or ending of a scene with a song. Only the female figures sing songs, in which they express their feelings. Prasād also comments on the importance of the female actors and the fact that their beautiful singing has contributed to the success and popularity of classical Sanskrit theatre.[9] The lyricism of the songs has prompted Gaeffke to talk about "lyrical drama" in Prasād's case.[10] Innovative for modern Hindi drama is the fact that Prasād writes his songs in Hindi, thus differing from Bhāratendu, who composed the lyrical parts of his plays in Braj.

Lakṣmīnārāyaṇ Miśra (b. 1903)

In the following, I will discuss Miśra's first social play, *Sanyāsī (The Ascetic)*, 1929.[11] It consists of four acts and handles the problems of romantic love and traditional marriage that became topical in Indian society during the 1920s under the influence of Western education and way of life. The drama deals with the problems of marriage and love. The two figure constellations, as represented by Kiraṇmayī, Dīnānāth and Murlīdhar on the one side, and by Māltī, Viśvanāth and Ramāśaṅkar on the other, serve to illustrate the two opposite views about which Miśra's contemporaries were debating.

With the spread of the British educational system, mixed school classes, in which girls and boys studied together, came into being. This brought about changes in the social structure of Indian society of the 1920s and 1930s. The traditional institution of the arranged marriage was "threatened," as the new social freedom in colleges made friendship between boys and

---

[9] ibid. 99-104

[10] See P. Gaeffke, *Hindi Literature in the 20th Century: A History of Indian Literature*, vol. VII.5 (Wiesbaden: Otto Harrassowitz, 1978) 99.

[11] Lakṣmīnārāyaṇ Miśra, *Sanyāsī* (Nayī Dillī: Vāṇī Prakāśan, 1993).

girls of marriageable age possible. The phenomenon of "romantic love" became a menace to the marriage regulations of conservative Hindu society.

Thus, young Māltī and Viśvanāth are fellow students in love with each other. When the jealous Ramāśaṅkar makes Viśvanāth's love letter to the young girl public, he disgraces her. In the second act, Māltī's father asks the student to marry his daughter. However, Viśvanāth refuses, as he has already vowed his life to the national independence of India. He is not ready to assume responsibility for his love for Māltī. He writes to her that she should accept marriage with another man. Cynically enough, he understands his decision not to marry her as a form of self-sacrifice and an expression of his socialist ideas:

> She is a Hindu girl...She cannot act against the will of her society and her parents. We care about society but not about the individual...We are real socialists. (*Sanyāsī*, 85)

Māltī comes to the conclusion that she does not want a romantic relationship with Viśvanāth, but marriage that will sustain the test of time. As she tells Viśvanāth in the last act, he has fallen in love with her because she was young, beautiful and from a good family. She asks whether this is love and why he did not marry her when her father asked him.

When she accepts Ramāśaṅkar's proposal, Kiraṇmayī, who has loved her whole life the inaccessible Murlīdhar, tries to make her reconsider her decision. Māltī, however, understands her acceptance of Ramāśaṅkar not as a defeat, but as a victory of the female sex over the male one. She says that she will marry him because of her own needs, and not to submit herself to him.

> You think that I have fallen...but I think that I am rising - I need a man to live with...to satisfy my own needs... Today the female sex won a victory over men's vainglory. (*Sanyāsī*, 101)

Māltī's and Kiraṇmayī's situations are similar. They will both cherish forever the memory of the man they have loved first and who has not married them. They have both married an older man, whom they do not love, but who has assumed the responsibility of taking care of them, providing them with a home, social life and security. Kiraṇmayī will never get over her dream of her romantic love for Murlīdhar and will always be unhappy with her husband, hating both him and herself for making a compromise. Māltī, on the contrary, realizes the necessity of making a compromise and of forgetting her love for the young and unreliable Viśvanāth, wishing for a stable marriage with Ramāśaṅkar.

The author implies that Māltī's way, which is the way of tradition and common sense, is the only possible way for an Indian woman to be happy. He supports his views by showing the nobility and understanding of Kiraṇmayī's husband, Dīnānāth, who feels her pain and is full of compassion for her. Moreover, the author makes Kiraṇmayī ask her husband for forgiveness, thus acknowledging that she has been mistaken in her rejection of him. With his play, Miśra supports the ideals of orthodox Hinduism and traditional Indian marriage, suggesting that the new social network, which has come into existence under British influence, will destroy the harmony and order of Indian society.

In this sense, the motif of the national movement for Independence from the British appears to be of secondary importance in the play and serves to illustrate the necessity of preserving the primordial Indian way from the dangerous influence of Western culture. In the author's eyes, the Indian way is better and has more to offer. Europe has wounded mankind and it is the task of Asia, as the mother of religion and civilization, to heal these wounds. (*Sanyāsī*, 79)

Bhuvaneśvar Prasād Śrīvāstav (1912/14–1957)[12]

Bhuvaneśvar wrote one act plays in which he explored the difficult relationship between man and woman. In *Pratibhā kā vivāh* (*Pratibhā's Marriage*), 1933,[13] eighteen-year-old Pratibhā decides to marry an old, widowed friend of her father's, Prakāś Varmā, although her father is against

[12] It is not certain whether Bhuvaneśvar was born in 1912 or in 1914. For more information, see Rājkumār Śarmā, "Bhuvaneśvar kā jīvan-vṛtt," *Bhuvaneśvar sāhitya*, Rājeśvar Sahāy Bedār and Rājkumār Śarmā, ed. (Śāhjahāṃpur: Bhuvaneśvar Prasād Śodh saṃsthān, 1992) 285-6.

[13] Bhuvaneśvar, *Bhuvaneśvar sāhitya*, Rājeśvar Sahāy Bedār and Rājkumār Śarmā, ed. (Śāhjahāṃpur: Bhuvaneśvar Prasād Śodh saṃsthān, 1992).

it, and the young Mahendra loves her and wants to marry her. She loves the young man, too, but tells him that she cannot marry him, as their feelings for one another are bound to disappear shortly after their marriage. In making her decision, she considers the old man's arguments that:

> My land and property, money, everything will be Pratibhā's, she will have a special place in society; she will be no non-existing housewife and mother but a respectable widow. She will have good contact with society and life, as she will have a past in society, people will know her because they have known her husband... (*Pratibhā kā vivāh*, 58)

Varmā is of the opinion that motherhood is a tedious profession. He says that he would not like Pratibhā to be forced to sell her body and youth and become a mother in order to earn her living. That is why he would like to marry her and offer her a better life. Mrs. Jośī, who has an intimate relationship with Pratibhā's father, tells him that Varmā had also asked her to marry him. She has not accepted because he had asked her on the deathbed of her husband. She considers not motherhood, but widowhood an insult to woman. It is implied that, as Varmā is much older, it is likely Pratibhā will become a widow soon. The young Pratibhā, however, does not share this view, and makes up her mind to marry the old man and transform her love for Mahendra into a brotherly-sisterly relationship.

In the context of Indian literature, this is a rather unusual interpretation of motherhood as a burden to woman. Being a mother is considered important to womanhood. Most Hindi playwrights, for example Māthur in *Koṇārk* (*The Temple of Konark*), 1951, and Rākeś in *Āṣāṛh kā ek din* (*One Day in the Month Aṣāṛh*), 1958, see motherhood as the only way out for a woman in a difficult and unhappy love relationship. It is regarded as the only possibility for her self-realization in society.

Bhuvaneśvar's interpretation, however, should not be understood as a defence of widowhood. It is rather that he is interested in his female characters not as mothers, but as women, who are in an antagonistic relationship with men. Thus, Pratibhā will not marry her beloved, as she is afraid of losing his love with the progress of time. No matter how absurd this argument might sound, Pratibhā's decision not to marry Mahendra is an attempt to keep their love intact. She does not fear marrying Varmā, however, as she does not love him, and is willing to engage in an antagonistic and destructive love-hatred relationship with him.

As Amarnāth, from the one act play *Romāns: romāñc* (*Romance: Horripilation*), 1935, puts it:

> If a man and a woman have lived together for two years and never fight, then both of them are cowards or they are both deceiving each other ... Happiness in married life is just a name for the vanity which expresses itself in the woman's victory over the man or of the man's victory over the woman. (*Romāns: romāñc*, 91-2)

Māyā in *Lāṭrī* (*Lottery*), 1935, is also intent on winning a victory over the men in her life. She is flattered to think of herself as a medieval princess, for whom two men are fighting. In her opinion, a pistol or a sword will decide the dispute between her husband Kiśor and her lover Pradyum. However, Pradyum does not want to take part in this "lottery" and leaves. But Māyā does not need the second man any more. She has already won her victory as a woman: "The real life of a woman starts only then when a man has ruined himself for her. This man could be either her husband or her lover." (*Lāṭrī*, 103)

Bhuvaneśvar's understanding of man and woman as engaged in a constant battle with each other is very similar to Strindberg's views on this matter, as reflected in the dramas *The Father*, 1887, *Play with Fire*, 1892, or *Dance of Death*, 1900, and anticipates Aśk's interpretation of this issue in the plays *Taulie* (*Towels*), 1943, and *Añjo Dīdī* (*The Elder Sister Añjo*), 1955. In Aśk's dramas, though, there is no eternal triangle. The "battle of the sexes" concerns only husband and wife. In Strindberg's *Play with Fire* and in *Dance of Death*, and in Bhuvaneśvar's plays, we find the same constellation of one woman and two men. Both authors have their heroines discuss their relationships with other men freely with their husbands, which is another instance of the influence of Strindberg and Western dramatic tradition on modern Hindi drama. In this respect, Bhuvaneśvar's portrayal of the female characters and their freedom to choose or change a partner is unprecedented in modern Hindi drama, where it is normally men who are depicted as enjoying more sexual freedom. By contrast, women are presented as waiting for them at home, in chastity and with devotion.[14] Bhuvaneśvar's portrayal of women does not reflect the objective reality of Indian society of the 1930s and 1940s, but is rather an expression of the author's artistic quest.

The dramatist does not depict woman only as a vile creature and a menace to men, as Strindberg did. Bhuvaneśvar also shows much sympathy and understanding for his female characters. In *Romāns: romāñc*, Amarnāth considers woman a problem for man and says that the only way to avoid this problem is to make her pregnant. The playwright, however, implies that he does not agree with this view by letting the main protagonist, Mr. Siṃh, say that "I consider woman a power, she is the one who makes life complete. Without her life would be like leaning on a blind man for support." (*Romāns: Romañc*, 92)

The author sees the problems as resulting from the antagonism between the sexes. He considers the primordial sexual instinct an all-pervading and often destructive force, especially in the age of sexual freedom. The play *Ūsar* (*Fallow Land*), 1938, deals with the power of this sexual drive. It can make one ill or unhappy, although one does not know the real reason for it. Sometimes hidden wishes or true facts, known only to our subconscious mind, can be revealed involuntarily.

The opening scene begins with a conversation between a householder, *gṛhasvāmī*, and a tutor. The man had been married for twenty-two years. It is vaguely suggested that his wife does not feel very well. The host ridicules the young man because he considers himself superior to the other inhabitants of the house and charges that he is conducting an intellectual experiment with them. The householder's wife (*gṛhasvāminī*), a fat young woman (*moṭī ramṇī*) and three young girls come home from a walk in the park. They all decide to play a game in order to pass the time. One of them mentions words and the others have to write immediately the things they associate with the words "room," "electricity," "perambulator" and "sex." The husband's answers are "responsibility," "brain," "marriage" and "science" respectively. His wife associates the word "room" with "bathroom," "electricity" with "darkness," "perambulator" with "baby" and

[14] The only two exceptions I could think of as regards the period discussed, are Aśk's one act play *Khiṛkī* (*Window*) and Rākeś's *Ādhe adhūre* (*Incomplete Halves*). In both plays, it is suggested that the female character had had a relationship with another man.

"sex" with "Shah Nazaf Road." They are all perplexed and the husband is very disquieted.

All of a sudden, the tutor appears and asks the boy whether he has seen his dictionary. The boy is surprised to find out that the tutor has been on the veranda all the time. He asks him whether he has talked to his father. The tutor answers that his father had said that the coming generation would be a better one than theirs, no matter whether they were cats or snakes. Surprised, the boy goes away to join the others. The final scene shows only the tutor on stage, lighting a cigarette.

The woman's answers reveal that there is something about her sexual dreams or married life that she has kept a secret from her husband. She has tried to suppress her thoughts in her subconscious mind, but the spontaneity of the play discloses them. There is something in her married life that makes her unhappy. The author does not make it clear whether it is a lost baby or an intimate relationship with another man or sexual dissatisfaction with her husband. The dramatist's psychoanalytic approach in the presentation of the woman's inner world implies that the real reason for her feeling of discontent is the incompleteness of her sexual and married life, about which she cannot talk, but can only keep to herself. The insertion of the associative game in the play enables the author to employ the technique of the "Freudian slip," the unconscious use of words motivated by and revealing of the subconscious mind, in order to disclose the woman's inner thoughts.

A question arises about the meaning of the title: why is the play called *ūsar* or "fallow, barren land"? Does it refer to the woman's loss of a baby or is it a reference to the barrenness of her dreams and sexual wishes that were never gratified at home? Bhuvaneśvar's psychoanalytic, Freudian approach in shaping a figure's character is innovative and unprecedented in the history of modern Hindi drama during this period.

The play *Ūsar* is also interesting on another level of interpretation. What is the function of the tutor, who appears at the beginning of the play to talk with the man and once again, at the end of the play, to tell his son the gist of their conversation? How can we explain his presence during the game, which remains unknown to the others? Was the game part of his intellectual experiment with the inhabitants of the house? And how is the father's statement that the next generation will be better than theirs to be interpreted? What is its connection with the game or with the other events described? Why does it have to appear at the end of the play, as if it conveyed some deep truth or climax?

The author employs dramaturgical techniques influenced by Western dramatical school that differ from Prasād's approach in a radical way. There is no action but only a situation in Bhuvaneśvar's plays, which is to be explained partly by the fact that he writes one act plays.[15] Similar to Miśra's dramas, the open ending of his plays does not provide us with any ready solutions to the questions raised. What is new and unusual in his dramatic technique is the unexpected, abrupt, explosive and paradoxical conclusion. Thus, Pratibhā's decision to marry old Varmā in *Pratibhā kā vivāh*, the departure of the lover Pradyum, who does not want to take part in the deadly "lottery" in *Lāṭrī*, or the woman's unexpected strike in *Sṭrāik* (*Strike*), 1938, and the puzzling ending in *Ūsar* illustrate this point clearly. Only a close reading of the plays enables us to find a clue to their interpretation and to see the hidden, second layer of the situation presented. Similarly, the casual mentioning of the tutor's intellectual experiment in the opening scene of *Ūsar* contains the clue to the hidden, second level of interpretation of the drama.

Bhuvaneśvar's use of everyday Hindustani language develops further Miśra's endeavors to emancipate modern Hindi drama from the all-pervading influence of Prasād's Sanskritized and learned vocabulary, and thereby create an understandable, natural and accessible dramatic language in Hindi. In this respect, Bhuvaneśvar's linguistic achievement prepares the ground for Aśk's approach to language. The two interpretative levels, the psychoanalytic approach, distinctive subject matter and the anomalous situations, unexpected abrupt open endings, absurdist elements in Bhuvaneśvar's plays, and the employed dramatic language are innovative for modern Hindi drama and anticipate many aspects in Aśk's dramatic work.

---

[15] Modern drama criticism postulates the opposition of action and situation as one of the differences between the full-length and the one act play. Cf. Gerhard Neumann, "Einakter," *Moderne Literatur in Grundbegriffen*, ed. Dieter Borchmeyer and Viktor Zmegac (Tuebingen: Max Niemeyer Verlag, 1994) 102-9. Nevertheless, there are many one act plays, which differ from their full-length counterparts only in the different number of scenes and acts. For instance, many of J. Māthur's, R. Varmā's and Aśk's one act plays disclose actions, and not situations. Therefore, Bhuvaneśvar's approach is innovative.

Bhuvaneśvar can be seen as the first *mature* recipient of the influence of Western dramatic tradition and intellectual thought on modern Hindi drama, including Strindberg's work and Freud's ideas. Therefore, his work is one of the indigenous dramatic sources that have inspired and contributed to the formation of Aśk as a playwright. In this respect, it should be pointed out that Aśk valued Bhuvaneśvar's work and included the one act play *Sṭrāīk* in an anthology of one-act plays he edited. In the preface to *Paccīs śreṣṭh ekāṅkī*, the author mentions Bhuvaneśvar at least three times, stating explicitly that he liked the plays *Ūsar* and *Sṭrāīk* very much.[16]

Jagdīścandra Māthur (1917–1981)

Jagdīścandra Māthur concentrates on fundamental questions of human existence, such as the purpose of art and the union of the individual with the Supreme. He sets the action of his plays against the background of the ancient and medieval history of India, and uses motifs from the *Purāṇas* and other mythological sources. In his one act plays, he addresses topical issues, for example the question of women's education and views on marriage perspectives among educated girls.

The action of the one act play *Bhor kā tārā* (*The Morning Star*), 1937,[17] is set in the Gupta capital Ujjayinī in the 5th century A.D. In the first scene, the poet Śekhar learns from his friend Mādhav that emperor Skandagupta values his poetry very much and has called him to his court to appoint him royal poet. Mādhav himself must go with Chāyā's brother Devdatt to fight against the Huns in Takṣaśilā. Mādhav thinks that now that Śekhar's art has received due recognition, there will be no obstacles to his marrying his beloved Chāyā. In the second scene, Śekhar and Chāyā are happily married. The young poet tells his wife that she is his poetry. He shows her the epic he has just completed, entitled *The Morning Star*. He started working on it on the day of their marriage and it is about their love for one another. At this point, Mādhav arrives and tells them that the Huns have attacked Takṣaśilā

[16] U. Aśk, ed. *Pratinidhi ekāṅkī* (Ilāhābād: Nīlābh, 1969) 77-95. See U. Aśk, preface, *Paccīs śreṣṭh ekāṅkī* (Ilāhābād: Nīlābh, 1969) 13. 18. 21.

[17] J. Māthur, "Bhor kā tārā," *Bhor kā tārā* (Ilāhābād: Nīlābh, 1957) 125-47.

and that Devdatt has died the death of a hero. He says that the country needs every citizen as a soldier to fight for freedom, and asks Śekhar to go throughout the country and speak to the people. With the power of his poetry, he could motivate the men and women of the Gupta kingdom and mobilize them for the coming war.

Śekhar burns his work *The Morning Star* and leaves Chāyā and his home in order to speak to his countrymen. Chāyā blames Mādhav for taking her morning away. He reassures her that he has not done so.

> Chāyā, I have not taken away your morning. It will be morning now. Up to now Śekhar has been just a morning star. Now he will be the morning sun. (*Bhor kā tārā*, 147)

The author implies that art should be purposeful and should serve a national cause in order to have aesthetic value. No matter how strong Śekhars's love for Chāyā is and how beautiful his romantic epic is, the artist must leave his home and write poetry for the ordinary people. Through his work, he should respond to the problems of life in order to become a true poet and leave a contribution behind. Māthur also codes this message in the pun used in the title of the play. The Hindi expression *bhor kā tārā* means not only "morning star" but also "transient, something that has momentary existence." Thus, by making Mādhav refer to the romantic poet of the past as a "morning star" and to the socially committed artist of the future as a "morning sun," the author implies that only purposeful art can last.

Māthur explores the idea of the relationship between art and its creator further in his play *Koṇārk* (*The Temple of Konark*), 1951.[18] It consists of three acts, set against the background of 13th century A.D Orissa. The first act serves as an exposition to the story. The sculptor Viśu cannot complete the temple of the Sun Deity in Konark. The spire cannot be adjusted on the lotus figure on top of the main body of the edifice. Because King Narasiṃhdev is engaged in a war with the Greeks, his minister rules Orissa. There is no end to the minister's despotism and the suffering of the people. Viśu thinks that this should not be their concern as they are artists and their task is to complete the temple. Thereupon, the sculptor reminisces about the past and tells Dharmpad the sad story of his youth. Twenty years ago, he

[18] J. Māthur, *Koṇārk* (Ilāhābād: Bhārtī Bhaṇḍār, 2018 vi.).

had abandoned his beloved when she told him that she was expecting a child.

Eighteen-year-old Dharmpad, who is very talented in his work, criticizes Viśu's artistic concept. The experienced sculptor says proudly that this is not just a temple, but metaphor for the course of life. It epitomizes mankind's activities, longings and pleasures. According to Dharmpad, there is one more step between the beginning of life and its exaltation, namely life's struggles. The sculptures of the temple tell nothing about the workers' pain and the sweat of their labor. Viśu believes that, as artists, they should not interfere with worldly affairs. Dharmpad is of the opposite opinion:

> ... it is also not appropriate that the sculptor should continue creating images of youth and amorous playfulness in a cool and protected corner when all around him the flames of atrocity and famine keep on growing. (*Koṇārk*, 26)

At this point, the minister himself appears on stage, threatening to cut off the sculptors' hands if the temple is not completed within a week. Only Dharmpad knows how to complete the spire.

In the second act, king Narasiṃh arrives to admire the gorgeous temple. He has won a victory over the Greeks, but has come without his army, as he could not wait to see the marvel of the Koṇārk temple. It turns out that Narasiṃh knows nothing of his minister's misdeeds. He annuls all the orders given in his absence. At this point, they find out that armed men are coming from all sides to attack the temple. Narasiṃh realizes that his minister has formed a plot against him. Dharmpad organizes the defence of the temple, just as Viśu discovers that Dharmpad is his son.

In the last act, Dharmpad is killed and the workers lose the battle. Thereupon, Viśu addresses the Sun Deity:

> You are the protector of my entire world; But how can I forget that I am your creator?... Koṇārk cannot be the symbol of the defeat of the sculptors. You and I together will not let this happen... No. (*Koṇārk*, 64)

The minister penetrates the temple with his men. Viśu roars with laughter and destroys the spire. The gigantic image of the deity falls down while the temple of Koṇārk collapses, thus causing the death of both its creator and invaders.

Similar to *Bhor kā tārā*, Māthur asserts in his play *Koṇārk* that art should be about life and the pain and sufferings of the ordinary people. The author implies that it is grotesque to build a temple that glorifies love and amorous activities when one is surrounded only by injustice and despotism. It is no coincidence that Dharmpad, who believes in creating purposeful and socially committed art, is the one who manages to complete the temple. He is not only the opponent to Viśu's ideas about the mere aesthetic value of art, but is Viśu himself, or more precisely, what the sculptor used to be when young. The enthusiasm and idealism of his youth live on in Dharmpad. The bond of blood only seals this close relation between them.

Since the temple in Koṇārk has become a symbol of real life, of the workers' sufferings, hopes and their struggle for freedom and against oppression, it cannot become a symbol of their defeat. Viśu destroys his own creation, thus taking revenge for the others' death and winning a final victory over the oppressor. The artist's life work is completed. The sculptor achieves final liberation in union with his creation. The building of the temple was his own life; its destruction his own death.

Māthur wrote the play in conformity with the requirements of naturalistic dramaturgy, thus, it can be presented very easily on stage. The action is concentrated, the plot is linear and the locale does not change. The drama starts with an *upakram* ("prelude") and ends with an *upsaṃhār* ("epilogue"). This stylistic device is borrowed from classical Sanskrit drama. The lyrical beginning of the play is an introduction to the story. The three voices that come from the background sing about the creation of the temple of Koṇārk. Similarly, the elegiac epilogue harmonizes with the mood of gloom and mourning at the end of the drama. In his notes to the stage director, Māthur points to the importance of having at least one female performer in the lyrical prelude and epilogue in order to compensate for the absence of female characters in the play.[19]

In the play *Pahlā rājā* (*The First King*), 1969, the dramatist even introduced the figure of the *sūtradhār* ("stage manager of a dramatic performance") who appeared in classical Sanskrit plays to introduce the different episodes and to explain new developments in the action. Māthur's use of different stylistic devices from classical Sanskrit theatre is not

[19] See J. Māthur, "Nirdeśak aur abhinetāoṃ ke lie saṅket," *Koṇārk*, by J. Māthur (Ilāhābād: Bhārtī Bhaṇḍār, 2018 vi.) 71.

antithetical to the naturalistic character of his dramaturgy. These elements enrich his plays and contribute to their Indian coloring without impairing the author's basic dramaturgical concept, which is oriented toward the successful presentation of his plays in a proscenium theatre. Māthur's use of various stylistic devices derived from classical Sanskrit drama differs from Prasād's artistic concept. The author's work has clearly been influenced by Western dramatic tradition.

Mohan Rākeś (1925–1972)

In his play *Ādhe adhūre* (*Incomplete Halves*), 1969,[20] Mohan Rākeś explores the man-woman relationship and gender roles in a 1960s middle-class Indian family. The setting of the drama is a contemporary household. The events happen in the house of an unspecified *Strī* ("woman") and *Puruṣ ek* ("man number one"). There are no clearly defined acts, but two long episodes with an interval between them. The locale remains unchanged throughout the play.

The play begins with the words of the man-in-a-black-suit, who functions as a narrator. He points out the typicality and universality of the characters and events portrayed. The role of the narrator is restricted to this one single appearance throughout the entire drama.

The opening scene shows the tired *strī*, or Sāvitrī, coming home from work and finding the whole house in a chaotic condition: the tea set is still on the table and her husband's clothes are scattered all over the house. When her husband appears on stage, their interaction resembles a quarrel more than a real conversation. Their married elder daughter, *baṛī laṛkī* ("big girl"), arrives and tells them about her problems at home. She feels estranged from her husband Manoj and has come home to find out what makes her feel so worthless. The parents have great difficulties in starting a conversation with their daughter. Their attempts are cut short by the appearance of the younger daughter, *choṭī laṛkī* ("small girl"), who comes with her own problems and complaints. The mother gives vent to her anger about being the one who has to do all the work in the family. Thereupon, the

[20] Mohan Rākeś, *Ādhe adhūre* (Naī Dillī: Rādhākṛṣṇa Prakāśan, 1969).

father leaves his home in protest. Sāvitrī tells the children not to worry, as he will be back by tonight. After that, the mother tries to reason with her son, *laṛkā* ("boy"), and make him understand that he needs a new job. She has invited her boss over to ask him to help them to find employment for the boy. *Strī* complains that she is like a machine that works for them all.

The boss, *puruṣ do* ("man number two"), arrives. He talks absent-mindedly about many topics and keeps on mixing up people and facts about them. He cannot remember her request concerning the boy, but promises to help. His only concern seems to be the strike in his company. The characters talk past each other, and not to each other. The boy has drawn a caricature of the guest and blames his mother for inviting her boss's salary, social status and good name, and not the man himself. Sāvitrī feels entirely misunderstood and complains that neither her husband nor her children appreciate her efforts. She decides to start a new life, taking care only of herself from now on.

The second part of the drama begins with a conversation between *baṛī laṛkī* and *laṛkā.* They comment on the fact that their mother put on her best *sāṛī*. To them, she looked as if she had made a serious decision. *Strī* has a date with her old friend Jagmohan, who is *puruṣ tīn* ("man number three"). She is thinking of leaving home and starting a new life.

When *puruṣ cār* ("man number four"), who is the husband's friend Junejā, arrives to meet the woman, he must wait for her. Upon the woman's return, they start a serious conversation about her married life. Sāvitrī tells him about all the things she hates in her husband, for example that he is not a strong personality but a failure in life. She complains of his being constantly under the influence of his friends and being rather dominant at home. Junejā, on the other hand, holds that *puruṣ ek* could have achieved more if she had not proven to him constantly how small and unimportant he was. He tells her that she respects other men simply because they are not her husband. But if she had married any of them, she would have started regretting choosing them anyway after some time:

> The truth is that if any of those other men in your life were in Mahendra's place, then you would begin to feel in one or two years that you married the wrong man. (*Ādhe adhūre*, 106)

Then he proceeds to tell her how her date with Jagmohan was. How he has probably said that he cherished the memories of the past, but could not commit himself to her now, as he had a new job, and she had children and a family, etc. Junejā makes clear to her that she has no choice.

Although Junejā has come to bring the couple together, he decides to persuade Mahendra not to return home. In the woman's eyes, there could be no reconciliation. The author reveals that she sees clearly that all men are the same, although they may look differently: "You are all the same. You wear different masks, but the face? The face of all of you is one."

In the final scene, the boy enters with his father, who has decided to return home after all. As he has just suffered a blood pressure attack, he is very weak and can hardly walk. His children rush toward him to help him into the house.

Mahendranāth and Sāvitrī's family is a new type of family. It is a nuclear family that has broken with the tradition of the classical Indian joint family. It is also a family where the traditional gender roles are changed. Thus, the mother of the house works, whereas the father mostly stays at home, as his attempt to start a business of his own has failed. They quarrel with each other constantly and are unhappy.

Rākeś shows that this is a family where nothing functions. The husband does not help with the work in the household and his wife is always overloaded with work, tired and unhappy. Nobody seems to take care of the little girl. She is portrayed as capricious and speaks to her elders disrespectfully. Moreover, she is accused by others' parents of spoiling their children with talk about sex. These accusations allude to the chaotic and unhealthy climate in the little girl's home. The boy is also unhappy. He would rather leave his home, but is unable to stand on his own feet and find a job that would enable him to be independent. The elder sister has married in order to flee from her home. She cannot be happy with her husband, as she feels that there is something about her childhood and youth in her parents' house that is always in the way.

It seems that, as a consequence of the break with the traditional institution of the joint family, life in Mahendranāth and Sāvitrī's house is chaotic and unhappy. The husband tries to compensate for the lack of a bigger family by sticking to his friends, for instance to Junejā. This is exactly the point that his wife cannot accept and criticizes. Though she works, she is not a career woman. She has an unimportant position in a firm and is entirely dependent on her boss. Although she had to accept the bitter truth that her husband turned out to be a failure in business, she has ambitions as regards her son. She does her best to find a job for him and invites her boss to her house for this purpose. When her son, however, tells her bluntly that he does not think much of her efforts and of her respect for her boss's salary and status, she decides to change her life. She meets her former friend and tries to start a relationship with him anew. It turns out that he is not ready for commitment any more and she must come back to her home and her previous life. As Junejā puts it, she has no choice.

Though she is ambitious and hard-working, she cannot think of changing or bettering her life on her own. In her eyes, all the high and attractive posts she seeks for her husband or for her son are meant for men, not for women. She seeks for realization through the men in her life, be it her husband, her son, her boss, her friend Jagmohan or her daughter's husband Manoj.[21] The changed gender roles do not imply a real change in society or better opportunities for women. That is why Sāvitrī has to continue to depend on the men around her and be unhappy instead of organizing her life according to her own wishes.

Rākeś does not seem to question this point. Though the woman is at the center of the play and we sympathize with her throughout, there is a shift toward the man's point of view at the end of the drama. The playwright makes us believe that it is the woman's aspiration for the new, the different and the inaccessible that accounts for the problems. A parallel can be made to Aśk's play *Bhaṃvar* (*Whirlpool*), 1961. Sāvitrī is at the center of the play, surrounded by four men. Similarly, Pratibhā is the central figure, surrounded by three admirers. Rākeś's heroine is already married whereas Pratibhā cannot find a husband to her liking. Nevertheless, their situations are very much alike. It is suggested that they are both unhappy, because they cannot accept reality. Instead, they desire men that remain inaccessible to them. However, whereas Pratibhā's conflict is within herself and due to her own intellectualism, Sāvitrī's conflict is with her husband. This is similar to Añjo's problem in Aśk's play *Añjo Dīdī* (*The Elder Sister Añjo*), 1955, and Laura's and Alice's conflict in Strindberg's plays *The Father* (1887) and *Dance of Death* (1900) respectively.

[21] It is suggested that Sāvitrī had had an affair with her daughter's husband before their marriage. (ibid. 107-8)

There is an important difference between Rākeś's interpretation of gender relationships and that of Strindberg, Bhuvaneśvar and Aśk. Whereas the last three authors see the battle of the sexes as innate, as pertaining to the nature of man and woman, Rākeś considers it to be the result of changes in gender roles in contemporary Indian society. This conveys a rather negative view of the question of women's emancipation. Rākeś's stance is quite opposite to the treatment of the subject by Aśk. In the play *Svarg kī jhalak* (*Glimpse of Paradise*), 1939, Aśk criticizes the fear men have about marrying an emancipated woman and starting a family in which gender roles might be changed.

An additional difference in Rākeś's presentation of the nature of the relationship between man and woman is the fact that he sees no possibility of communication between the sexes. Though Strindberg, Aśk and Bhuvaneśvar have seen the conflict between man and woman as a never-ending and deadly battle of the sexes, their protagonists can communicate with each other. They quarrel, fight, and destroy each other, but talk *to* each other. Language is their strongest weapon! In Rākeś's play, real conversation is not possible any more.

The characters talk *past* each other and not to each other. Vasudha Dalmia is right in observing that the play reflects a total breakdown of communication.[22] Husband and wife cannot talk to each other any more. They cannot carry out their conflict in a verbal debate. The only real verbal controversy that takes place in the drama is not between the two spouses but between the woman and Junejā, the husband's proxy.[23] This points to the impossibility of dialogue.

Children and parents fail to communicate as well. Neither the mother nor the father can start a conversation with their eldest daughter when she asks them to. The girl feels estranged from her husband. She attempts to talk to her parents about it, as she cannot communicate her feelings to her husband. (*Ādhe adhūre*, 24-7) The visit of the woman's boss is another example of failed communication. Though many topics are mentioned, nothing is really said. The boss utters words to fill in the time. He is not interested in the

---

[22] See Vasudha Dalmia, "Neither Half nor Whole: Dialogue and Disjunction in the Plays of Mohan Rakesh," *Tender Ironies: A Tribute to Lothar Lutze*, ed. Dilip Chitre et al. (New Delhi: Manohar, 1994) 184.

[23] ibid. 196.

woman's family at all. He cannot remember their previous conversation and mixes up people and events. Even the first minutes of Sāvitrī's meeting with Jagmohan are marked by their inability to start a conversation. The external reason might be the constant coming and going of the children. The real reason is that they have grown apart from each other throughout the years.

The breakdown of communication finds expression in ways other than the fragmented dialogue. There is no real action in the drama, only events that are revealed through the figure's utterings. The characters are not round any more and they convey the idea of being fragmented selves, torn from others and from their environment. Dalmia compares the play to Handke's *Kaspar*. I also consider *Ādhe adhūre* structurally close to Samuel Beckett's *En attendant Godot* (1953), or its English version, *Waiting for Godot* (1955). In Beckett's play, we find the same breakdown of communication, which expresses itself in the fragmentation of dialogue and the lack of action. Estragon and Vladimir talk past each other rather than to each other. They are estranged from their fellow human beings, from themselves and from their environment.

When talking about the structural similarities between the two plays, we should keep in mind their differences in theme. Beckett's play is not simply about our inability to communicate with each other and about being lost in a world that is not ours any more. It is also about the meaning of life, our hopes and fears. Estragon's and Vladimir's eternal waiting stands for the hope (or hopelessness?) of the human condition. It is about a time when mankind has lost its beliefs, ideals, and its faith in God and the purposefulness of the universe and of our lives. By contrast, Rākeś's play centers on the more immediate gender problems of contemporary Indian society.

Rākeś's dramatic work can be seen as another example of the creative impact Western dramatic tradition had on modern Hindi drama. His play *Ādhe adhūre* is innovative, as it treats new subject matter and uses dialogue in a way no Hindi playwright had ever used before. Thus, it represents a rethinking of the convention of a round character and questions the very notion of action in a play.

Chapter Two

Upendranāth Aśk

Life and Literary Biography

Upendranāth Aśk was born on December 14th, 1910, in Jalandhar, Punjab. His family was Bhārdvāj Brahmans of the Sārasvat Gotra and belonged to the lower middle class. Aśk is the second of the six surviving children of the family. His childhood and youth were spent in great poverty and in constant fear of his father, Paṇḍit Mādhorām, who was an alcoholic and used to beat his children and wife. Aśk's mother, Basantī Devī, was illiterate; however, she was the pillar of the family. The children learned from her how to endure their father's beatings without losing their courage and hope of a better future.

Aśk passed his B.A. examinations at the Dayanand Arya Vedic College in Jalandhar in 1931. One year later, he married his first wife Śīlā Devī and worked as a teacher in his native town. In 1933, he accepted a position as a writer in Shimla. He had to ghost write a book on newborn children for his employer Harnām Dās. This job was a deep disappointment to Aśk: the promised good working and living conditions proved to be very bad and the agreed royalty was not paid in full. Aśk then moved to Lahore to study law. He worked as a journalist and a translator for different newspapers, among them Lālā Lājpat Rāy's Urdu newspaper *Vande Mātaram.*

In 1936, Aśk passed his L.L.B. examinations and wanted to become a judge. His wife died of tuberculosis, leaving behind a son. Shaken by her death, Aśk gave up his ambitious plans for a career as a judge and decided to dedicate himself entirely to writing. In 1939, he left for Preetnagar (today's Amritsar) in order to contribute to the Hindi-Urdu edition of *Prīt-Laṛī*. In 1941, Aśk married for the second time, but abandoned his wife Māyā Devī only after two months. Half a year later, he married his third wife Kauśalyā and started working as a dramatist and an adviser at All India Radio. He was also the editor of the Hindi edition of *Sainik Samācār*. In 1945, he moved to Mumbai (Bombay) to work as a scenarist for Filmistān.[1] Aśk played in two films, *Mazdūr* (*The Worker*), produced by Nitin Bos, and Aśok Kumār's *Āṭh Din* (*Eight Days*). The dialogues he wrote for *Mazdūr* were awarded the prize for best dialogue of an Indian film in 1945. The next year Aśk fell ill with tuberculosis and spent two years at the "Bel Air" sanatorium in Panchgani.

With the help of the honorary payment of Rs 5000 awarded to him and the Hindi poet Nirālā because of their illness, the author settled down in Allahabad in 1948. To the end of his days on January 19th, 1996, he worked there as a freelance author. Almost all his books were published in his private publishing house, Nīlābh Prakāśan, which was founded by his wife Kauśalyā in 1949.

Aśk's first poem was published in 1926, when he was sixteen years old. His first collection of short stories in Urdu, *Nau Ratan* (*Nine Jewels*), appeared in 1930. The author's first penname was 'Śanāvar' ("An Expert Swimmer"). In order to pay homage to his deceased wife, he changed it to 'Aśk' ("Tear") and started publishing all his works under the name of 'Upendranāth Aśk.' In 1933, Premcand wrote the preface to Aśk's second collection of short stories *Aurat kī Fitrat* (*Woman's Nature*), thus acknowledging the young author as a promising writer.

In the beginning, Aśk wrote in his mother tongue Punjabi. Later on he switched over to Urdu. In the preface to *Paccīs Śreṣṭh Ekāṅkī (Twenty-Five Best One-Act Plays)*, he states that he wrote in Urdu from 1929 to 1946.[2] From 1933-34 onwards he followed Premcand's advice and started using

[1] Filmistan is the center of the Indian film production industry in Mumbai (Bombay).

[2] U. Aśk, "Hindī ekāṅkī aur jīvant raṅgmañc: Ek lambī ḍhalān ke donoṃ chor," *Paccīs śreṣṭh ekāṅkī*, by U.Aśk (Ilāhābād: Nīlābh, 1969) 1.

Hindi as a means of literary expression. However, it took years before he felt confident about his Hindi. Up to 1946, he composed the first draft of his literary production in Urdu and translated it carefully into Hindi afterwards. Many of Aśk's works, which date from this period, have both Urdu and Hindi titles.[3]

In 1947, his first novel *Girtī Dīvāreṃ (Falling Walls)* was published. It made Aśk famous and encouraged him to work on the other six novels of the *Girtī Dīvāreṃ*-series.[4] This was a task that he pursued to the end of his life. The 1940s and 1950s witnessed a tremendous dramatic production as well. Most of his one act plays were published in the anthology *Paccīs Śreṣṭh Ekāṅkī*, 1969. Similarly, a collection of short stories *Sattar Śreṣṭh Kahāniyāṃ (Seventy Best Short Stories)*, 1958, bears witness to the author's quest in the field of modern Hindi short story writing. His five volume memoirs *Cehre: Anek (Faces: Many)*, 1977–1988, is a vivid document of contemporary literary life and people. Aśk talks about himself in the third person and comments on his times and his fellow writers from the viewpoint of this [presumably] detached literary persona.[5]

The legacy of the author's literary career spans sixty years, comprising fourteen novels, fourteen collections of short stories, eleven plays, eight collections of one act plays, and ten anthologies of poetry. Aśk also published eight books of memoirs, six collections of interviews and four volumes of essays. He wrote four monographs on literary criticism, edited four anthologies and translated seven books into Hindi.[6] As regards the

---

[3] This is true of many of his plays. The Urdu titles of some dramas are as follows: *Kaid-e-hayāt (Kaid), Parvāz (Uṛān), Subah śām (Añjo Dīdī), Azlī rāste (Ādi mārg), Farzānā (Bhaṃvar)*.

[4] The *Girtī Dīvāreṃ* cycle consists of: *Girtī Dīvāreṃ (Falling Walls)*, 1947, *Śahar meṃ Ghūmtā Āīnā (A Mirror Wandering in the City)*, 1963; *Ek Nanhī Qindīl (A Tiny Candle)*, 1969, *Bāndho na Nāv is Ṭhāv (Don't Tie the Boat in this Place)*, 1974, *Palaṭatī Dhārā (The Reversing Stream)*, 1996, *Iti Niyati (And Thus is Fate)*, unfinished and unpublished. Apart from the *Girtī Dīvāreṃ* cycle, Aśk wrote seven more novels.

[5] *Cehre: Anek* is full of personal attacks and negative remarks regarding many of Aśk's contemporaries. The fact that the author possessed his own publishing house and the ensuing lack of censorship led to his practice of discussing personal matters between himself and his literary "enemies" both in his memoirs and in the prefaces of many of his books.

[6] Some of Aśk's novels, short stories and their translations in English, German and Russian have already been referred to in the introduction to this volume.

totality of the author's oeuvre, the observation was made that Aśk is the only writer of modern Hindi whose work represents so many different genres. Thus, his work can be compared to the encyclopedic literary production of Bhāratendu and Premcand.[7]

What are the social and literary circumstances relevant to the making of the writer Aśk?

The author's social background, the social status of his family, his difficult childhood and the death of his first wife, all prompted him to write in a realistic way and to portray the life and suffering of the ordinary people surrounding him. His fellow writers with whom he associated and the movements of the Hindi literary scene of the 1930s and 1940s have doubtlessly played a significant role in his further development as a socially committed author of realism. In this sense, the collection of short stories of "naked realism" by the Urdu writers of the 'Aṅgāre Group' should be mentioned. Aśk's contact with the Hindi-Urdu authors Kṛṣṇa Candra and Rājendra Siṃh Bedī and his correspondence with Premcand are also important. These writers are considered the great realists of modern Hindi-Urdu literature.[8]

The 1930s and 1940s marked an important phase in Aśk's literary career. During these years, Aśk matured as an author. It was also the time when the Progressive Writers' Association (PWA) and the Indian People's Theatre Association (IPTA) were founded, two events that influenced Hindi literary writing and criticism considerably.

The Indian Progressive Writers' Association (IPWA) was founded in 1935 in London. The founders were Indian students influenced by Marxist literature and the modernist Bloomsbury group.[9] The Urdu writer Sajjad

---

[7] "Aśk: saṅkṣipt jīvan paricay," posthumous edition [Ilāhābād: Nīlābh, n.d] 2.

[8] Not only Premcand but also Udayśaṅkar Bhaṭṭ and Harikṛṣṇa Premī were close to Aśk and encouraged him to write in Hindi. While working for All India Radio in Delhi, Aśk associated with the Urdu writers Maṇṭo, Khvāzā Ahmad Abbād, Faiz Ahmad Faiz, Mīrājī and Rāśid. He often had to deal with the Hindi authors Jainendra, Ajñeya, Banārsīdās Caturvedī and Girijā Kumār Māthur. The literary discussions, readings and talks, the entire artistic atmosphere, which surrounded Aśk, have contributed to his development as a realistic author. See "Ciṭṭhī-pātī," *Aśk 75*, vol.2 (Naī Dillī: Rādhākṛṣṇa, 1986) 359-420; K. Aśk, ed. *Aśk: Ek raṅgīn vyaktitva* (Ilāhābād: Nīlābh, 1961).

[9] Famous members of this group were Virginia and Leonard Woolf, Clive and Vanessa Bell. Other literati, who frequented the meetings, were E.M. Foster, T.S. Eliot, and Arthur Waley.

Zahīr and the English language author Mulk Raj Anand were among them. One year later, the first meeting of the All India Progressive Writers' Association (AIPWA) took place in Lucknow. It was organized by Sajjad Zahīr and chaired by Premcand, who talked on the purpose and meaning of literature in his opening address. The journal *Haṃs* served as a forum for progressivist ideas.

What is characteristic of the progressivist literary scene?

The progressivists believed that writing can bring about social change and can improve society. The Progressive Writers' Association was founded to offer ideological and theoretical support to authors who strove for a realistic presentation of life and its problems in their works. Its proponents wanted to emancipate modern Hindi literature from dependence on traditional subjects such as the union and separation of the hero (*nāyak*) and heroine (*nāyikā*). In the beginning, this shift of emphasis, from the preoccupation with the emotional to a closer exploration of the economic reasons for our human condition, was productive. It resulted in significant works of literature that studied the many backward institutions of contemporary Indian society. It also tried to effect reforms by offering severe critiques and solutions in the spirit of socialist realism and Marxism. In this sense, much attention was given to women and their suffering.[10]

However, later on, the increase of dogmatism and political propaganda (many progressivist authors were adherents of the communist party) and the strong tendency of progressivist criticism toward prescriptivism, caused

---

This was a group of friends with Cambridge affiliation, who lived in the squares and streets of Holborn known as Bloomsbury. The Apostles' Society in Cambridge, of which Virginia Woolf's father, Sir Leslie Stephen, was a member, is a direct ancestor of the Bloomsbury group. The Bloomsbury members not only translated non-Western works, but published and supported unknown non-Western writers. Without E.M. Foster's help, Mulk Raj Anand might have never seen his novel *The Untouchable* published and might have committed suicide in his despair. For more information on the contribution of the Bloomsbury group to non-Western literature, see Suzanne Henig, "The Bloomsbury Group and Non-Western Literature," *Journal of South Asian Literature* 10 (1974-75): 73-82. In her dissertation, Anne Daisy Rockwell points to Mulk Raj Anand's account of his contact with the Bloomsbury group, *Conversations in Bloomsbury* (New Delhi: Oxford UP, 1995). See A.D. Rockwell, *The Novelty of Ashk: Conflict, Originality and Novelization in the Life and Work of Upendranath Ashk*, diss., U of Chicago, 1998 (Ann Arbor: UMI, 1998) 9832167. 58.

[10] Yaśpāl's novel *Jhūṭhā Sac (False Truth)*, 1958-60, is exemplary in this respect.

many authors to feel more restricted than encouraged in their realistic writing by membership in the Progressive Writers' Association. Some authors, for example U. Bhaṭṭ, Dinkar and Baccan, gave up their membership. Similarly, the founding of the Parimal Society in Allahabad should be seen as a reaction to the growing dogmatism and restrictive prescriptivism of Indian progressivism.[11] On the other hand, we should not underestimate the importance of progressivism to the Hindi literary scene. Literati, who were not affiliated with the Progressive Writers' Association, were also influenced by its ideas. In this respect, we can point out Sumitrānandan Pant's and Bhagavāticaraṇ Varmā's work.

The Indian People's Theatre Association (IPTA) was founded in 1941 in the hope that it would help to create a living Indian theatre, able to challenge the commercial Parsi theatre and educate an interested audience. Indeed, some 600 plays by progressive authors were staged in the first five years of the existence of the Indian People's Theatre Association.[12]

At this time in the history of Hindi literature, Indian literati were divided along the lines of ideological affiliation. If one was a progressivist, it was unthinkable one could be a member of the "decadent" Parimal Society as well. The case of Aśk is most interesting. He was associated both with the Indian People's Theatre Association and with the Progressive Writers' Association. He was also the chair of the Allahabad Artist Association, and

---

[11] In 1944, this new literary club, which was named "Parimal" after Nirala's collection of poems, was founded in Allahabad. The writers Dharmvīr Bhārtī, Lakṣmīkānt Varmā, Nareś Mehtā, Ajñeya, Prabhākar Mācve, Rāmsvarūp Caturvedī, Jagdīś Gupta, who belonged to the Parimal Society, were criticized for creating art for art's sake. However, a closer look at their writing will show that they did not endeavor to escape the purposefulness of literature pursued and propagated by the prcgressivist discourse, but strove after more freedom of expression. Characteristic of their ideas were openness toward Western thoughts and literature and experimentation with new techniques. The Parimal Society of Allahabad existed some twenty-five years and held about four hundred literary *goṣṭhīs* ("seminars"). It cultivated the fine art of the coffee house tradition of literary discourse, for which Allahabad became famous among literati throughout the Hindi area. See Karine Schomer, *Mahadevi Varma and the Chayavad Age of Modern Hindi Poetry*, (Berkeley: University of California Press, 1983) 146-9.

[12] See S. Potabenko, "K istorii razvitija sceničeskoj dramaturgii i teatra chindustani," *Literatury Indii: Sbornik statej*, ed. I.S. Rabinovič and E.P. Celyśev (Moskva: Izdatel'stvo vostočnoj literatury, 1958) 105-48. IPTA staged Aśk's one-act play "Tūfān se pahle" in Allahabad in 1951. (See P. Gaeffke, *Hindi Literature in the 20th Century: A History of Indian Literature*, vol. VII.5 (Wiesbaden: Otto Harrassowitz, 1978) 95.

was in contact with the Parimal Society that saw itself as ideologically opposed to the Progressivists.

I will therefore proceed to examine the ideological implications of the issues of literary influence and literary tradition in the example of Aśk's controversially received position in the Hindi world of letters. The special case of this representative author illustrates clearly the ideological controversies of the time.

The writer's political impartiality in a time of severe ideological polarity on the Hindi literary scene was unusual. His contacts both with the Progressivists and with the Parimal Society were interpreted as due to the author's lack of social orientation and as an expression of his anti-progressivist stand. Aśk was compelled to pronounce his views openly, and did so at a PWA meeting in 1972. In his address, he emphasized the writer's freedom to embrace different ideas and to be independent of ideologically biased restrictions on his work.

I consider Aśk a representative of Indian progressivism not because of his personal proclamations, but because of the evidence provided by his literary work. The author portrays the social evils and conservatism of Indian society in an attempt to reform it. Women's difficult situation and their unfair treatment by modern Indian society is a central issue in his work. In his plays, Aśk pleads for an improvement of women's existence through education and emancipation. The author's message is unmistakably "progressivist." The metaphors he uses, his distanced tone and the open endedness of his works, which do not provide us with ready solutions to the problems discussed, do not undermine the purposefulness and the social commitment of his work. Rather, this innovative style helps his work escape the prescriptivism and clichés of contemporary progressivist literature. Moreover, it questions the legitimacy of our operating with labels like "progressivism" when studying an author.[13]

Aśk's literary work indicates that he should be considered a progressivist author who escaped the dogmatism of the later development of Indian Progressivism. As a novelist and a writer of short stories, he continued the

[13] The relativism of using names of movements when studying an author becomes even clearer when considering the fact that Aśk's dramatic method, with its realism and open-ended quality, was influenced both by progressivist literature and by Western naturalistic theatre.

democratic, realistic and socially committed literary tradition of Hindi, as manifested in the works of Premcand, Yaśpāl, and Kṛṣṇa Candra.

How does the issue of influence refer to the *dramatist* Aśk?

Hindi dramatic tradition was indebted for its origin and development to Western theatre. Bhāratendu's plays would not have been possible without the influence of Western drama. This influence concerned mainly a new dramatic form, meant for a new type of theatre, namely, the proscenium theatre.

In the preface to his representative collection of one-act plays, *Paccīs śreṣṭh ekāṅkī* (*Twenty-Five Best One Act Plays*), 1969, Aśk points out that he had not been influenced by Indian dramatic tradition.[14] However, there are many similarities between Bhuvaneśvar's and Aśk's interpretation of gender. The author wrote in conformity with the dramaturgical innovations of Western theatre that were first introduced into modern Hindi drama by Miśra and Bhuvaneśvar. Though Miśra's and Bhuvaneśvar's work could not contribute to Aśk's formation as a dramatist the way Chechov's, Ibsen's and Strindberg's plays did, I consider these two Indian playwrights important as Aśk's predecessors.

While denying the influence of Indian dramatic tradition on his work, Aśk points to his great indebtedness to Western drama for his formation as a playwright.[15] Indeed, Aśk's personal library bears witness to his excellent knowledge of Western drama. The author's impressive collection of books of Western and Indian literature, which comprises hundreds of volumes in English, Hindi, Urdu and Punjabi, can be found in his study in Allahabad. The numerous marked pages in Aśk's copies of Western dramatists' works reveal the author's close reading of Western drama. The translations of three of O'Neill's most representative plays are a further proof of his interest in Western theatre.[16]

---

[14] See U. Aśk, "Hindī ekāṅkī aur jīvant raṅgmañc: Ek lambī ḍhalān ke donoṃ chor," *Paccīs śreṣṭh ekāṅkī*, by U.Aśk (Ilāhābād: Nīlābh, 1969) 6-24.

[15] ibid. 10-24.

[16] Aśk translated O'Neill's *Long Day's Journey into Night*, 1956, *Beyond the Horizon*, 1920, and *Mourning Becomes Electra*, 1931. Nīlābh Prakaśan published the Hindi translations in 1992.

The Dramatist Upendranāth Aśk

With his first play, *Jay Parājay* (*Victory and Defeat*), 1937,[17] Aśk follows in the influential dramatic tradition of Prasād. This historical play consists of 200 pages, and many acts and scenes. The dramatic figures represent exceptional people who are kings, princes and princesses. It is also the first Hindi drama to be successfully staged.[18] Nevertheless, Aśk decided never again to write historical plays. In his opinion, the times required dramas that discussed social problems and addressed contemporary society directly.

Aśk dedicated himself to the writing of social plays, thus continuing the tradition set by Miśra. Among Aśk's social plays, we can distinguish dramas on topical socio-political issues of contemporary Indian society and plays that treat the problems of a typical lower middle-class Indian family.

In the plays on socio-political subject matter, the author exposes backward religious practices and their impact on society. For example, in the one-act play *Ādi mārg* (*The Primordial Way*), 1943, as well as the drama *Alag alag rāste* (*Separate Ways*), 1954,[19] Aśk reveals the conflict between tradition and modernity. The author criticizes the conservatism of orthodox Hinduism and argues that new times require a rethinking of traditional religious practices.

In the one act play *Camatkār* (*Marvel*), 1941,[20] the dramatist shows how progress is hindered by the many superstitions in which the ordinary people are sunk. The author exposes the superficial and commercial approach to religion. He criticizes his more educated contemporaries who stimulate people's innocent belief in marvels only to make money and to sell their products, in this case a medicine.

---

[17] U. Aśk, *Jay parājay* (Ilāhābād: Nīlābh, 1984). A summary of the play is found in the introductory part of S. Rastogī's essay. See S. Rastogī, Bhūmikā, *Jay parājay*, by U. Aśk (Ilāhābād: Nīlābh, 1984) 10-40.

[18] See P. Gaeffke, *Hindi Literature in the 20th Century: A History of Indian Literature*, vol. VII.5 (Wiesbaden: Otto Harrassowitz, 1978) 101.

[19] U. Aśk, "Ādi mārg," *Ādi mārg: cār sāmājik nāṭakoṃ kā raṅgmañc saṃskaraṇ*, by U. Aśk (Ilāhābād: Nīlābh, 1961) 11-59; ——, *Alag alag rāste* (Ilāhābād: Nīlābh, 1986).

[20] ——, "Camatkār," *Mere priya ekāṅkī*, by U.Aśk (Ilāhābād: Racnā, 1975) 183-204.

In the play *Andhī galī* (*Blind Alley*), 1956,[21] Aśk unmasks the corruption of the officials responsible for the refugees' misery after India's partition in 1947. This is partly an autobiographical drama, for it reflects the difficulties Aśk's family experienced as refugees. The narrative elements of the play make it one of the first instances of epic theatre in Hindi. It consists of seven independent episodes related by shared protagonists.

In the one act play *Tūfān se pahle* (*Before the Storm*), 1946,[22] Aśk criticizes the power play of politicians who exploit the religious feelings of the people in order to achieve their own political ends. Greedy for power, the politicians instigate religious fanaticism, inciting the hatred and cruelty that marked the Hindu-Muslim relations at the time of India's partition. The result was bloodshed and the death of millions of innocent people.

Aśk's critique of contemporary Indian society is individualized through the example of the effect that the failure of the religious, administrative and political systems has on individual persons and fates. In conformity with Indian literary tradition and similar to Eugene O'Neill, many of whose dramas Aśk translated into Hindi, the family unit is at the center of the author's individualism, not a single person.

In the play *Chaṭhā beṭā* (*The Sixth Son*), 1961,[23] the author discusses the figure of an authoritarian father and the ensuing conflict between father and son. Noteworthy is the employed expressionist dramaturgical technique of partial substitution of the action with scenes of dream and memory. In this way, Aśk intensifies the collision between illusion and reality. The same technique is used in Arthur Miller's *Death of a Salesman*, 1949, which handles, among other issues, the difficult relationship between father and son.

In the plays that explore another thematic point of emphasis, namely the relationship between man and woman in marriage, family happiness is also illusory and transitory. Similar to Strindberg, Aśk studies the subject of the battle of the sexes for power and dominance. In the play *Añjo Dīdī* (*The Elder Sister Añjo*), 1943,[24] he shows that it can end in a deadly way. The one

---

[21] ——, *Andhī galī: nātak ke kṣetra meṃ ek nayā prayog* (Ilāhābād: Nīlābh, 1956).

[22] ——, "Tūfān se pahle," *Paccīs śreṣṭh ekāṅkī*, by U. Aśk (Ilāhābād: Nīlābh, 1969) 265-91.

[23] U. Aśk, "Chaṭhā beṭā," *Ādi mārg: cār sāmājik nāṭakoṃ kā raṅgmañc saṃskaraṇ*, by U. Aśk (Ilāhābād: Nīlābh, 1961) 176-263.

[24] U. Aśk, *Añjo Dīdī: do aṅkoṃ kā ek sāmājik nāṭak* (Ilāhābād: Nīḷābh, 1983).

act play *Taulie* (*Towels*), 1943,[25] illustrates how absurd and, at the same time, how important the petty everyday quarrels about the use of the towels at home can be. It is impossible for the partners to change or for the differences to be smoothed over. Only the partners' readiness to compromise could save their marriage.

Female characters are at the center of the plays on family issues. In the dramas *Ādi mārg* and in *Alag alag rāste*, Aśk emphasizes the necessity of women's emancipation by showing how difficult and humiliating their situation in contemporary Indian society can be. In the one act plays *Lakṣmī kā svāgat* (*Lakṣmī's Welcome*), 1938[26] and *Pāpī* (*The Sinner*), 1937-8,[27] the author exposes the double standards of conservative Hindu society and the heartless way in which women are often treated.

Similar to Ibsen, as an advocate of women's rights, in the plays *Ādi mārg*, *Alag alag rāste* and *Kaid aur uṛān* (*Prison and Flight*), 1950, the author sees a possible solution in the emancipation of women through education and more independence. In the one act play *Carvāhe* (*The Herdsmen*), 1942,[28] Aśk's heroine elopes with her beloved, thus asserting her right to make her own decisions and to be happy.

On the other hand, the dramatist deals with the problems of the educated and emancipated woman in a traditional non-emancipated society. She cannot start a family, as the men, who feel attracted by her, are also afraid of her and decide to marry a poorly educated and traditionally brought up woman in the end. In the plays *Svarg kī jhalak* (*A Glimpse of Paradise*), 1939, and *Bhaṃvar* (*Whirlpool*), 1961,[29] Aśk implies that the emancipation of the entire society is a prerequisite for a happy relationship between men and women.

In his play-within-the-play dramas, the author attempts to destroy theatrical illusion and experiments with new stage forms. Innovative

---

25 ——, "Taulie," *Paccīs śreṣṭh ekāṅkī*, by U. Aśk (Ilāhābād: Nīlābh, 1969) 79-102. An English translation of the play is available. See U.Aśk, "Towels," *Indian Literature* 24/3 (1981): 65-83.

26 U. Aśk, "Lakṣmī kā svāgat," *Pacīs śreṣṭh ekāṅkī*, by U. Aśk (Ilāhābād: Nīlābh, 1969) 291-305. A Russian translation of the play is available. See N.A. Viśnevskaja, *Indijskaja odnooktnaja drama* (Moskva: Nauka, 1964) 170-80.

27 U. Aśk, "Pāpī," *Paccīs śreṣṭh ekāṅkī*, by U. Aśk (Ilāhābād: Nīlābh, 1969) 449-65.

28 U. Aśk, "Carvāhe," *Paccīs śreṣṭh ekāṅkī*, by U. Aśk (Ilāhābād: Nīlābh, 1969) 57-77.

29 ——, *Svarg kī jhalak* (Ilāhābād: Nīlābh, 1971); ——, *Bhaṃvar* (Ilāhābād: Nīlābh, 1961).

techniques in the plays *Nayā purānā* (*New and Old*), 1948, and *Pardā uṭhāo! Pardā girāo!* (*Raise the Curtain! Drop the Curtain!*), 1950,[30] are reminiscent of Thornton Wilder's and Samuel Beckett's dramatic approaches in *Our Town*, 1938, and *Waiting for Godot*, 1953, respectively. In *Pardā uṭhāo! Pardā girāo*, Aśk ridicules the lack of professionalism on Hindi stage. In *Nayā purānā*, we get involved in the story Aśk tells about Lilī's wedding jewellery, which her mother has entrusted to Lilī's teacher Devcanda, only to find out at the end of the play that this was not a real play but just a rehearsal. The stage director, who has been sitting quietly all the time, watching the play and smoking his cigarette, suddenly interrupts the performance in the end and says that he does not consider the play worth staging, as the story presented is not realistic. Though the stage manager in Wilder's *Our Town* plays a more active role by being also the commentator of the drama, one cannot fail to notice the similar approach of the two authors to destroy the theatrical illusion by introducing the figure of the stage director. In this respect, Aśk's play *Nayā purānā* has been influenced by Wilder's drama.[31]

---

[30] —, "Nayā purānā," *Tūfān se pahle*, by U. Aśk (Ilāhābād: Nīlābh, 1972) 81-103; —, *Pardā uṭhāo!Pardā girāo* (Ilāhābād: Nīlābh, 1971). A Russian translation of the last play is available. See N.A. Viśnevskaja, *Indijskaja odnooktnaja drama* (Moskva: Nauka, 1964) 180-94.

[31] In his article, Buddruss points to another source of influence for the play *Nayā purānā*, namely A. Milne's drama *The Man in the Bowler Hat: A Terribly Exciting Affair*. See G. Buddruss, "Zum Vorbild des Einakters 'Nayā purānā' von Upendranath Ashk." *STII* 7 (1981): 3-10.

Part Two

Western Tradition
and
Upendranāth Aśk's Dramatic Style

Chapter Three

Language and Characterization

In the following discussion, I analyse a limited number of formal structures of the dramatic text with regards to the message they communicate to the receiver of information. Structuralist criticism is indebted to Russian formalism for the distinction between literary and ordinary use of language and between story and plot, or fabula and sujet. Similar to Russian formalism, it considers the central function of ordinary language to be the communication to auditors of a message or information through references to the world existing outside of language. In this aspect, Roman Jakobson's model of verbal communication is of great importance. An additional common feature of Russian formalism, structuralism, and narratology is the analysis of the literary work as a self-sufficient verbal entity, independent of reference to the author and the replacement of the author by the reader as the central agency in criticism.

I discuss Aśk's plays from a structuralist perspective and follow the practice of structuralist critics who analyse literature on the explicit model of modern linguistic theory. I study the plays by taking into consideration the general aim of structuralist criticism to construct poetics that stands to literature as linguistics stands to language. Or to put it in the terms of narratology, to formulate the "grammar" of narrative in terms of structures that recur in many texts independently of the differences in the narrated subject matter.[1]

Dramatic Language

Dramatic Speech, Ordinary Language, Narrative Speech

Although both dramatic and ordinary speech are informed by dialogue as a means of communication, dramatic speech differs from ordinary speech in the fact that it has two addressees, the dramatic figure that participates in the dialogue and the audience. It also has two subjects, the fictional expressive subject manifested in the dramatic figure speaking and the real expressive subject, namely the author.

The main difference between narrative and dramatic speech is the immediacy of dramatic speech lacking the situational abstraction characteristic of narrative speech.[2] Thus, dramatic speech is always performative speech, i.e. by producing an utterance, a dramatic figure is actually performing an action. However, the identity of speech and action does not apply to every dramatic speech. In epic theatre, for instance, the introduction of commentative remarks, which aim at explaining an action, results in speech unrelated to action. Thus, epic elements attempt to compensate for the loss of a mediating communication system in drama and give dramatic speech a likeness to narrative speech.

---

[1] M.Bal, *Narratology: Introduction to the Theory of Narrative* (Toronto: U of Toronto P, 1985); S. Rimmon-Kenan, *Narrative Fiction: Contemporary Poetics* (London and New York: Methuen, 1983); M. Toolan, *Narrative: A Critical Linguistic Introduction* (London and New York: Routledge, 1988).

[2] See M. Pfister, *Das Drama. Theorie und Analyse* (Muenchen: Wilhelm Fink Verlag, 1988) 19-20.

Pfister illustrates this point by referring to Jakobson's communication model for narrative and dramatic texts.[3] Jakobson's model is based on an analysis of a dramatic text from the point of view of sending and receiving information. A literary text is therefore considered a communication network between a sender and a receiver of information. Whereas a narrative text consists of three communication systems, an external, a mediating and an internal one, a dramatic text operates only with two systems, an external and an internal one. [4]

As Jakobson's model shows, there is no fictional narrator or fictional addressee in drama. How does this fact affect the nature of dramatic speech? The loss of communicative potential in comparison to narrative texts is compensated for in two ways. In the first place, dramatic texts can rely on non-verbal codes and channels for transmitting information, such as setting, masks or costumes. In the second place, some aspects of the narrative function may be transferred to the internal system. For instance, by making the dramatic figures ask questions and give answers that are actually meant to inform the audience, reveal background information or characterize another dramatic person.

In this sense, the introduction of epic elements in modern theatre, such as the appearance of a commentator or producer, is another way to compensate for the limited communicative potential of dramatic texts. Authorial texts in the form of introductions, prefaces or extended stage-directions are equally important in the case of closet dramas and should be interpreted as another attempt to create a narrative medium within the dramatic text.

---

[3] ibid. 20-2.

[4] The internal communication system comprises the fictional characters in the work that communicate through dialogue. The mediating system includes the internal system, and the fictional narrator or narrative medium and the fictional addressee of the fictional narrator. The external system encompasses the previous two systems (in the case of drama only the internal system), and the author implied in the text, together with the implied ideal receiver of the whole work. According to Jakobson's model, the actual author and the actual reader are outside of the external system (ibid. 20-2).

Dramatic Speech and Figure Characterization

Another feature of dramatic speech is that it is one of the most powerful means a playwright has to characterize dramatic figures. How is dramatic speech, or verbal communication, related to the dramatis personae? What is the significance of language in the constitution of a dramatic figure? In drama, the receiver can perceive a figure as who it is only by means of what is said and how it is said. I will therefore proceed to study the relationship between verbal communication and the characterization of dramatic figures.[5]

The lack of a mediating system in drama limits the possibilities of characterization through language from an authorial perspective. Therefore, in order to characterize his personages convincingly, a playwright usually adopts a figure-oriented point of view, which relies on the explicit or implicit self-representation of a figure.[6] Thus, a dramatic person may portray himself in a certain light in his own words, explicitly, in the context of either monologue or dialogue, or implicitly, through the stylistic texture of his utterances.

An implicit self-representation is based on the social context in which the figure appears. In order to delineate a figure through language, it is important to state the qualities of individual speech. In the first place, we are faced with the question of whether a dramatic figure's language reveals features typical of a particular sociolect or idiolect, and whether figurative or literal speech is used, an abstract or concrete vocabulary. In this respect, we should ask about the type of sentences a figure uses (such as statements or questions). We should further inquire whether the sentence structures are marked by hypotaxis or parataxis and whether there is an emphasis on certain semantic groups. In the second place, a question arises about the way the speeches of different groups interact. In this sense, the length of a

---

[5] Pfister argues that whereas all the figures in French classical tragedy speak in the same kind of rhetorically elevated and metrical style, in naturalistic theatre, each figure is associated with its own personal verbal style. The author refers to the first case as absolute linguistic homogeneity, while the second is complete linguistic differentiation of dramatic speech. Two intermediary linguistic levels would be the use of typified class-oriented sociolects and the introduction of individual idiolects as a means of characterization (ibid. 178 -9).

[6] ibid. 176-80.

figure's speech, the frequency with which interruptions occur in the dialogue and the temporal arrangement of the various speeches, for instance whether the utterances occur successively or simultaneously, inform the implicit self-representation of a dramatic figure.

Thus, a lengthy speech reveals a more talkative person and a tendency toward monologues may point to the figure's egocentricity and desire to dominate. The more frequent the interruptions of the utterances are, the closer is the relationship between the dramatis personae. A sentence-structure marked by parataxis and the conjunction "and," in Hindi *aur*, is based on a consensus-dialogue. On the contrary, the use of hypotaxis and the frequent use of subordinate clauses and the conjunction "but," in Hindi *magar*, *lekin*, or *parantu*, reveals an utterance charged by conflict. Similarly, in a normal case, we would expect a figure's utterance to follow another figure's utterance. In this respect, the introduction of simultaneous speech or of pauses may point to disrupted communication between the personages. The use of figurative speech contributes to the illustration or concretization of a particular situation, thus directing the audience' attention in a certain direction. Imagery is also important on a thematic level of interpretation. The author enriches the thematic implications of the events by creating metaphorical models for the interpretation of the plot. Thus, the image of a storm or rain can characterize a figure by illustrating an unhappy human condition. It can also prepare the audience for a forthcoming catastrophe.[7]

In conclusion, we should point to the polyfunctionality of dramatic language. A dramatic utterance always fulfils several functions simultaneously, even though one of these may dominate the others in a particular instance. When my analysis focuses on one specific function, for instance on the referential function, which is related to the content of speech, it should be noted that I adopt this approach for the sake of clarity, and not because I disregard the polyfunctionality of dramatic speech.[8]

---

[7] In a theatrical performance, a figure may also be characterized implicitly by extralingual, or paralingual, qualities such as its voice quality, costume, and individual physical and personal qualities of the actor performing the role.

[8] Here is a brief summary of the functions to which Pfister refers. If the function is linked to the receiver, we talk of appelative function. This implies that the sender of information wants to address or influence the receiver of the message. If it is connected with the sender of

Aśk's Dramatic Language

In drama, the characters cannot be separated from their environment because they exist only in relationship to their surroundings. Therefore, information about the personages' fictional (social) context is essential for understanding a dramatic figure. Aśk is influenced by the aesthetic of Western naturalistic theatre that postulates linguistic differentiation of the dramatic figures' speeches as a means of characterization and individualization. Therefore, the author implements stylistic devices in order to adapt the characters' language to their social surroundings.

Dramatic Language and Fictional Context

Let us first ask the question: how does verbal communication help to reveal the fictional social context in which the figures appear? The figures' language is adapted to their particular social and individual situation. Thus, Aśk's dramatis personae speak a form of everyday Hindustani that is often colored by gender, or sociolect- and idiolect-specific features. The figures are characterized implicitly by gender-specific features. For instance, in almost all the plays, men address women by using the informal form for the second person plural, *tum*, whereas women employ the polite form, *āp*.

Besides, Aśk employs sociolect and idiolect specific linguistic features, such as the use of a dialect, foreign language or grammatically incorrect speech patterns in order to individualize his personages. Thus, in the drama

---

information, i.e. if the sender's character is reflected in the use of language, we think of expressive function. Whereas the referential function is connected with the speech content, the phatic function refers to the channel for transmission of information. The metalingual function is linked with the code of information. The poetic function expresses itself in presenting the message as verbal supersign. It is manifested in the way a message refers to itself and thus draws the audience's attention to its structure (ibid. 151-66).

Andhī galī, the Punjabi refugees speak in Punjabi. The author gives their words in the *devanāgarī* script and provides a translation of their speech in a footnote below the text.[9] Very often, dramatic figures who are Sikhs speak in Hindi, but their speech is interspersed with Punjabi words. In this case, only the foreign expressions are translated in a footnote.[10] Similarly, in the one-act play *Tūfān se pahle*, a Muslim character uses a predominantly Urdu vocabulary. In another context, a highly Urduized vocabulary points to the natural, everyday speech of a typical Indian family as well. For instance, in the drama *Añjo Dīdī*, the dramatis personae use words like *insān*, "human being," *zindagī* "life," *zulm* "tyranny" and *tilisma* "magic," not their Hindi counterparts, *manuṣya*, *jīvan*, *atyācār* or *māyā/ indrajāl*. The choice of words reflects the realistic linguistic situation in North India and contributes to creating the illusion of "naturalness."

Another sociolect and idiolect specific feature of Aśk's mode of characterization of the dramatic figures through language manifests itself in the fact that a less educated person's dialogue is marked by grammatical mistakes.[11] In the comedy *Batsiyā*, Hīrā speaks in incorrect Hindi with a strong Braj influence. These linguistic peculiarities of her utterances correspond to her lower social status as an uneducated cleaning woman. Similarly, Rāmgulām in the one-act play *Pardā uṭhāo, pardā girāo!* is a *caprāsī*, "peon," and speaks in the Braj dialect.[12] In contrast, the speech of an educated or wealthier figure is informed by the use of English vocabulary. If entire sentences are in English, the author provides a

---

[9] Cf. U.Aśk, *Andhī galī* (Ilāhābād: Nīlābh, 1986) 36. 37. 41.

[10] ibid. 37-8.

[11] Viśnevskaja values the social coloring of the dramatic figures' dialogue, but criticizes the insertion of dialectal words and grammatically incorrect sentence structures as means of characterization for less educated personages. See N. A. Viśnevskaja, *Indijskaja odnoaktnaja drama* (Moskva: Nauka, 1964) 125.

[12] Cf. U. Aśk, "Batsiyā," *Pardā uṭhāo! Pardā girāo*, by U. Aśk (Ilāhābād: Nīlābh, 1971) 156-7; ——, "Pardā uṭhāo, pardā girāo," *Paccīs śreṣṭh ekāṅkī*, by U. Aśk (Ilāhābād: Nīlābh, 1969) 43. 45. Although Braj is a language with a rich literary tradition, it should be noted that it is often looked upon as a dialect, as a regional language that is "inferior" to Hindi. Therefore, authors of modern Hindi literature often make their protagonists speak in Braj in order to imply their lower social and educational status.

transliteration of the English text.[13] The introduction of the idiosyncrasies of a child's language in *Andhī galī* is interesting and innovative for modern Hindi drama. The child, who cannot pronounce the sounds "na" and "ra," substitutes "la."[14] In this case, this technique does not aim only at a realistic portrayal of a child figure on stage. There is something pathetic about a little child, who cannot even pronounce the words properly yet, entreating the official to employ his brother. Thus, Aśk's emphasis on the idiolect specific features of a child's speech is meant to move the audience and alert it to the issues of unemployment and social injustice.

What is the nature of dialogue? What is the length of the speeches, what is the sentence structure? How do the different figures' dialogues interact in the play? Does the playwright use figurative speech in the dramas?

Linguistic Features of Dialogue

An examination of Aśk's plays shows that monological and lengthy dialogical speeches are very rare. This is the case even in the character drama *Bhaṃvar*, where the emphasis is on the heroine's inner conflict. The only exceptions are the plays *Kaid* and *Uṛān*. Thus, in *Kaid*, Dilīp and Appī have lengthier utterances in which they talk about their past relationship and difficult present. However, in the third act, the protagonists' dialogue is interspersed with long descriptions of the beauty of nature around them. The lengthier utterances in the first instance provide the audience with additional background information that is essential for understanding the nature of the conflict. In my opinion, in the second example, the length of the dialogues contributes neither to dramatizing the action nor to upholding the suspense that is necesssary for keeping the audience involved.

In *Uṛān*, Māyā expresses her views on partnership, marriage and love in dialogues that resemble monological speech. Her lengthy utterances characterize her as a serious but lonely person who is inclined to self-

---

[13] U. Aśk, *Andhī galī* (Ilāhābād: Nīlābh, 1986) 22; ——, "Batsiyā," *Pardā uṭhāo, pardā girāo*, by U. Aśk (Ilāhābād: Nīlābh, 1971) 170-2.

[14] ——, *Andhī galī* (Ilāhābād: Nīlābh, 1986) 82.

contemplation. They also enable the author to communicate to the audience his views on the subject extensively. The lengthy dialogues make the play appear more as a narrative work full of symbols than as a drama based on conflict.

The predominant syntactical structure of the sentences in Aśk's plays is hypotaxis. Thus, a typical sentence consists of a main clause and one or two subordinate clauses, linked with each other by the conjunctions *lekin* or *magar*, "but," and the conjunction *agar*, "if," or the relative pronoun *jo*, "who, which." The usual type of sentences in Aśk's dramas are statements, though questions are not uncommon. Questions prevail over statements only in cases where there is a stormy dispute between the figures. Thus, the dialogue between Trilok and Pūran in *Alag alag rāste*, in which the two men are presented as ideological opponents, and the utterances that reflect "the battle of the sexes" between partners, such as Vāṇī and Dilīp in *Kaid* or between Madhu and Vasant in *Taulie*, consist of many questions.[15] Similarly, in these dramas, the figures interrupt each other quite frequently. This linguistic feature points to the greater extent of intimacy between the dramatis personae, on the one hand, and, on the other hand, to a situation charged by serious conflicts.

However, no matter how stormy the disputes are, the temporal arrangement of the figures' utterances shows no disruption of communication. As already discussed, quite the opposite is the case in Mohan Rākeś's or Samuel Beckett's work. In Aśk's plays, one figure's utterance follows another person's dialogue. Even in the dramas that deal with the subject of the battle of the sexes, language is the partners' most powerful weapon. The characters never talk past each other. There are conflicts, but no disruption of communication.

Dramatic figures often use figurative speech as well. For instance, in *Kaid*, the servant Kiśansinh describes Appī's unhappy life by means of a metaphor. He refers to her human condition by using the word *kaid*, "prison."[16] In the same play, both Appī and Prāṇnāth refer to the image of King Kong, thus alluding to the film in which an ape takes a beautiful girl

---

[15] U. Aśk, *Alag alag rāste* (Ilāhābād: Nīlābh, 1986) 62-108; ——, *Kaid aur uṛān* (Ilāhābād: Nīlābh, 1972) 62-5; ——, "Taulie," *Paccīs śreṣṭh ekāṅkī* (Ilāhābād: Nīlābh, 1969) 84-91. 93-102.

[16] U. Aśk, *Kaid aur uṛān* (Ilāhābād: Nīlābh, 1972) 98.

away from her home against her will.[17] It is not difficult for the audience to grasp the author's message and to start identifying Prāṇnāth with King Kong and Appī with his victim. In this sense, the imagery enables the playwright to communicate the speech content of the figures' dialogue to the audience more vividly. Very often, Aśk gives his plays metaphorical titles, providing a symbolic meaning that illustrates the main theme. This is the case in the dramas *Kaid aur uṛān*, *Prison and Flight*, where woman's imprisoned human condition and her flight into independence are discussed. In *Svarg kī jhalak*, *A Glimpse of Paradise*, the author deals with the difficult nature of marriage by ironically referring to it as "paradise." Similarly, the play *Bhaṃvar*, *Whirlpool*, treats the subject of the chaos and illusions in Pratibhā's life, while *Tūfān se pahle*, *Before the Storm*, exposes the evils coming with the "storm," that is the religious fanaticism that caused the murderous Hindu-Muslim clashes.

An examination of the linguistic features of dialogue in Aśk's plays also allows us to look into the gender implications of dramatic speech. Thus, women talk more and longer than men in the dramas. Their utterances present them as active and dynamic. Most often, their emotions, thoughts and actions are essential to the further development of the dramatic conflict. It is not an exaggeration to say that, in most dramas, "things happen" when women speak. In this sense, dramatic speech enables Aśk to characterize the female figures as round and dynamic, while the male ones are flat and static.

Thus, Rānī's and Rāj's characters are central to the development of the conflict in *Alag alag rāste*. Conversely, their male counterparts, Trilok and Madan, play only a minor role. Similarly, in *Kaid and uṛān*, much attention is given to Appī and Māyā, whereas the male figures Dilīp, Prāṇnāth, Madan, Rameś and Śaṅkar are important only in terms of shedding light on the behavior of the female protagonists. In this sense, in *Añjo Dīdī*, Añjo is the active person in the household. She stands by her views and lifestyle and opposes Śrīpat, while her husband Indraṇarāyaṇ is characterized as a passive man who easily succumbs to the harmful influence of their guest. The most convincing example is provided by the drama *Bhaṃvar*, in which the female heroine is not only the protagonist, but also the central character in the conflict.

[17] ibid. 60.

Functions of Dialogue

The identity of action and speech in Aśk's plays is achieved by means of numerous linguistic features. For instance, the figures' utterances are not long and are written in an everyday Hindustani, in a vivid idiomatic language, often interspersed with imagery. In addition, the author employs dramatic speech to compensate for the lack of narrative medium in drama. Most often, the playwright reveals background information through the figures' utterances.[18] In this way, dialogue functions as an informative exposition. For instance, in *Kaid*, Appī's husband Prāṇnāth reminisces about the past in a conversation with his wife. Through his words we learn about all the past events that are relevant for understanding the conflict. Similarly, in the drama *Alag alag rāste*, the background information is mediated narratively, through the figures' speeches. In this case, the audience is presented with two informative expositions. In the first instance, Rānī and Rāj's father discusses with his guests his daughter's unhappy marriage. In this way, the audience becomes acquainted with Rānī's problems. In the second case, Rāj tells her sister the truth about her own marriage. As a consequence, we become aware of the real dimension of the dramatic conflict that enables us to follow its development in a more critical way.[19]

Besides, Aśk employs dialogue in order to characterize the dramatis personae. Most often a dramatic person is characterized by another person's utterances. There are no cases of explicit figure self-representation in Aśk's plays. A personage never describes his character in his own words. He is always portrayed either through his actions, inner thoughts and feelings or in the words of other figures. Thus, our opinion of Rānī's husband Trilok is based on her father's and her own utterances. Similarly, Rāj's characterization of Madan, which contrasts with that of her father, helps us to see the true nature of his character. To point out another example, in the

[18] Whereas Ibsen employed this technique in his plays at the end of the 19th century, thus establishing a new dramatic mode, Aśk's approach is innovative in the field of modern Hindi drama.

[19] Dramaturgically, the dramatic suspense is maintained and our critical reaction is encouraged by the employment of dramatic irony.

play *Añjo Dīdī*, Añjo's character is revealed in Indranārāyaṇ's and Śrīpat's dialogues. Similarly, Pratibhā's inner conflict and her fear of real earthly love are communicated to us in Hardatt's utterances on this matter. In this respect, it should be pointed out that Aśk characterizes his figures predominantly by means of dialogue.

In certain cases, dramatic speech functions as a medium through which the author communicates his ideas on a certain subject matter, like the plight of theatre in India or the nature of realism. Thus, in *Pardā uṭhāo! Pardā girāo*, Aśk criticizes the conditions under which amateur theatrical performances are prepared and performed. In the one-act play *Nayā purānā*, he makes the stage director and author of the play discuss its stageability. The producer rejects the play, as he does not consider it realistic. The short discussion between author and stage director provides a clue to Aśk's views on the issue of realism in art.[20]

Dramatis Personae: Figure Conception and Characterization

Dramatic Figure, Dramatic Person, Dramatis Personae, Dramatic Character, Figure Configuraion

In my study, the terms "dramatic figure," "dramatic person" and "dramatis personae" are used as synonyms, although the term "dramatis personae" refers to the sum of all the figures that appear in a play. Besides, it should be pointed out that many critics prefer the expression "figure," as it clearly points to the fictional nature of the characters.[21] Unlike natural persons, dramatic persons cannot be separated from their environment. A fictional figure is a deliberate construct and the fictional context defines the figure

[20] G. Buddruss, "Der Einakter 'Nayā purānā' von Upendranath Ashk," *STII* 2 (1976): 3-26.

[21] See M. Pfister, *Das Drama. Theorie und Analyse* (Muenchen: Wilhelm Fink Verlag, 1988) 221.

entirely.[22] The dramatis personae appear as people who portray themselves in the play. We perceive them in terms of the way they interact with others, and not as individuals, and they appear to us as speakers. The term "character" alludes to the contrasts and correspondences between the figures. It does not refer only to the distinguishing features of an individual figure, but to its interaction with the other personages, as reflected in the figure configuration.[23] A figure configuration can have either an expanding or repetitive structure.

In a configuration with an expanding structure, there is a progressive development, where the number of the persons expands in the beginning and diminishes toward the end. Most of Aśk's dramatic figures appear in this type of expanding configuration. To point out one example, in the drama *Alag alag rāste*, the opening scene shows Tārācand talking to his friend Śivrām. In the following scenes, with the development of the conflict and the complication of the action, more and more figures are introduced. This structure of figure configuration is typical of analytical drama,[24] where the conflict is resolved only in the end.

Conversely, in a repetitive configuration, there is a constant repetition of figure configurations. By repeating identical configurations the author can demonstrate the changes in the protagonist' development. For instance, in *Alag alag rāste*, Rānī and Rāj appear several times together, in the same configuration. Rānī of the first act is different from Rānī of the third act, who rejects her husband and even flees from her home. By making the two women always appear together in different situations and by making them share each other's thoughts and feelings, Aśk shows that the change that takes place in Rānī's character is also due to her involvement in her sister's conflict. Another instance of repetitive configurational structure is presented in the dramas *Kaid* and *Taulie*, where the two-figure configuration of the opening scene reappears in the final scene. Thus, in *Kaid*, Appī is shown to

---

[22] ibid. 221-2.

[23] ibid. 225-32. The section of the dramatis personae that is present on stage at any particular point in the course of the play is the configuration in which the figure appears (ibid. 235-40).

[24] Whereas the decisive event in conflict or goal oriented drama takes place only toward the end of the action that is presented scenically, in analytical drama this event has happened before the beginning of the presented action. In this sense, the progression of the action serves to reveal this past event.

be ill and apathetic both at the beginning and at the end of the play. Similarly, both the opening and the final scene of the one act play *Taulie* present Madhu and Vasant quarreling about the petty question of how to use towels at home.

The employment of figure constellations with repetitive structure is also connected with the cyclical composition and the open-ended quality of the plays. Through the repetitive figure configurations in the above-mentioned plays, Aśk implies the impossibility of change. Appī's human condition cannot improve, nor can Madhu and Vasant's marriage be transformed into a harmonious union. The conflict remains unresolved. Thus, the importance of the structure of the figure configurations for the development of the conflict shows clearly the dialectical relationship between plot and figure.

Figure Conception

Figure conception is a purely historical category and refers to the anthropological model that informs the construct of the dramatic figure. Thus, from a historical perspective, drama criticism distinguished between statically and dynamically conceived figures, between personification, type and individual. E.M. Foster introduced the concepts of "flat" and "round" character, while E. Bentley enriched the theoretical approach to figure conception by stating the differences between "open" and "closed" figure conception. In addition, Pfister distinguishes between transpsychological and psychological figure conception.[25]

A "flat character" is defined by very small, unified and homogeneous features. Everything the figure does or says points to this particular set of features the author has chosen to characterize it. Conversely, a "round" character is marked by a complex set of characteristics from different levels. The character is presented in interrelation with biographical and social circumstances, psychological disposition, and interpersonal relations. Each situation and the relation to every new figure that appears in the drama

---

[25] See M. Pfister, *Das Drama. Theorie und Analyse* (Muenchen: Wilhelm Fink Verlag, 1988) 241-50.

serves to reveal new sides of the character. Thus, the figure is presented as a complex unity of many different characteristics.

Whereas a figure conceived along the lines of personification embodies just one single quality or concept, the type encompasses a whole set of characteristics. When the author conceives a figure as an individual, he aims at showing clearly the features that are unique to that figure. He does so by concentrating on as many details as possible. The information presented refers to the figure's appearance, speech, behavior, biography, and social milieu. This type of dramaturgy is characteristic of naturalistic theatre.

The concepts of open and closed figure conception refer to the degree of information available to the audience for understanding a dramatic person. When the information provided is incomplete or when important pieces of information are deliberately omitted, the figure becomes enigmatic, i.e. this is a case of an open figure conception.[26] Conversely, when the figure is entirely defined by the author, no matter whether the information is explicitly or implicitly conveyed, we have an instance of a closed figure conception. Naturalistic theatre aims at this kind of closed, clearly defined figure conception.

Similarly, naturalistic dramatists conceive figures with a reduced level of awareness. The figures appear to behave naturally and are usually not able to discuss themselves explicitly, with self-awareness that is uncommon in real life. In this case, Pfister talks of psychological figure conception. When a figure is able to "discuss" itself, there is an example of transpsychological figure conception. In modern drama, there are instances, where a figures' reduced level of awareness is partly overcome by the presentation of exceptional situations, such as talking and visions in semi-sleep or in a drunken state of mind. This device enables the dramatist to reveal the workings of the figure's consciousness, or in other words, to increase its level of awareness.[27]

If we examine the figure conception in Aśk's plays, we will see its proximity to the dramaturgy of naturalistic theatre. The author conceives both his round and flat characters as individuals about whom he provides information on different levels. He brings out details from the figure's external appearance, age, biographical or social background, speech pattern,

[26] An instance of an open figure conception is Shakespeare's Hamlet (ibid. 246).
[27] ibid. 247-9.

and behavior toward other figures. This information is included either in the secondary text, in the stage directions describing the figure's appearance, or in the primary text itself, explicitly, in the dialogue, and implicitly, through the deliberate choice of a certain type of behavior, locale, costume, verbal behavior and stylistic texture.

Another feature of Aśk's dramatic style, which points to the author's proximity to the dramaturgy of the naturalists, is the employment of closed figure conception. As the examples above show, the author's dramatic figures are completely defined by the information transmitted to the audience. Not only the main protagonists, such as Appī and Māyā in *Kaid aur uṛān*, Pratibhā in *Bhaṃvar*, Raghu in *Svarg kī jhalak*, Rāj and Rānī in *Alag alag rāste*, and Añjo in *Añjo Dīdī*, but also other major characters, such as Prāṇnāth, Dilīp, Rameś, Śaṅkar and Madan in *Kaid aur uṛān*, Hardatt in *Bhaṃvar*, Umā in *Svarg kī jhalak*, Madan, Trilok, Pūran and Tārācand in *Alag alag rāste*, and Śrīpat, Animā and Indranārāyaṇ in *Añjo Dīdī*, are conceived by the author by providing all the information based on their biography, social context, verbal and interpersonal behavior, and physical appearance that could enable the audience to understand their characters and the motives for their actions.

For instance, the author provides detailed information about the locale connected with the figures or on their appearance in the secondary text. Thus, the interior of both Appī's and Añjo's houses is described in the stage directions at the beginning of the dramas. In *Kaid*, the chaos and untidiness of Appī's home and the late hour at which she is still in bed suggest her apathy and illness. Conversely, the orderliness in Añjo's house and the remark that this is not Indranārāyaṇ's but Mrs. Indranārāyaṇ's home point to Añjo's mania for cleanliness and order, and to her dominant position in the household.[28] In *Añjo Dīdī*, the dramatist describes the appearance of all the personages immediately before they come on stage. These descriptions provide information not only about the figure's physical looks; often, they offer a glimpse of their inner life or behavior. Thus, Animā is portrayed as a young woman of twenty-five, middle-sized, with a half-ripened body. As the audience will find out later, she is not married. In this respect, the remark about the "half-ripeness" of her body alludes to the incompleteness

[28] U. Aśk, *Kaid aur uṛān* (Ilāhābād: Nīlābh, 1972) 37-40; ——, *Añjo Dīdī: do aṅkoṃ kā ek sāmājik nāṭak* (Ilāhābād: Nīlābh, 1983) 23-5.

of her sexual life. Añjo is described as a thirty-year old woman who looks five years older than her age, and is busy only with the household. She is very serious, has wrinkles and does not smile. This physical portrayal matches her behavior, that of a pedantic person who takes life too seriously.

Similarly, the negligent way in which Śrīpat is dressed is suggestive of his excessively easy-going attitude toward any norms and rules. Thus, the author makes him appear in dirty, partly unbuttoned clothes. The expensive watch on his wrist and the cigarette in his mouth support this impression.[29] In the opening stage directions of the drama *Bhaṃvar*, Aśk provides biographical information about Pratibhā's past that helps us to understand her behavior and beliefs. Her unhappy first marriage, which was based only on physical attraction, left her disappointed and lonely and accounts for her distance from all the men around her and for her aspiration for a purely intellectual relationship with a man.[30] Thus, in the stage directions, the author has individualized the young woman not only by referring to her beauty, youth and education, but also by presenting important biographical details about her.

In addition, the author underlines the individuality of his personages by providing sufficient information about the figures' biographical and social background, as reflected in their verbal behavior. In this sense, the speech pattern of a Punjabi refugee differs from that of a middle-class employee or an educated judge.

Some figures are conceived only on the basis of their behavior toward the other dramatis personae. For instance, in *Alag alag rāste*, Madan never appears on stage. He is portrayed only through his misbehavior toward his wife Rāj. Although we never see Madan, we perceive him as an individual and can easily distinguish him from Trilok. This fact becomes even more apparent when we consider the one act version of the drama, the play *Ādi mārg*, in which neither Madan nor Trilok appear on stage. Nevertheless, they are conceived clearly as individuals, as the way they behave toward their wives is entirely individualized.

Most often, biographical information, which is essential to the conception of the figure as an individual, is provided explicitly, in the primary text. Thus, in the drama *Kaid*, we come to know the sad story of

---

[29] ibid. 24. 26. 33.

[30] ——, *Bhaṃvar* (Ilāhābād: Nīlābh, 1961) 51-3.

Appī's marriage through Prāṇnāth's reminiscences about the past. This information is transmitted to us in the dialogue between husband and wife.[31] Similarly, in the second act of the play *Añjo Dīdī*, Śrīpat's semi-monological utterance, when talking to Animā, reveals details about his life that help us to perceive him as an individual with a male-centrist viewpoint, who is afraid of commitment and whose relationships with women are marked by the desire to dominate them.[32] Similarly, in *Svarg kī jhalak*, information about Raghu's unhappy first marriage with a poorly educated woman is conveyed in his speech. This piece of biographical information is important to understanding his wish not to make the same mistake twice and marry an educated woman after the death of his first wife.[33] This biographical detail exposes his final decision to marry the uneducated Rakṣā as cowardice and personal failure to live up to his ideals. It should be noted that Aśk's critique of Raghu's decision illustrates clearly the author's views on marriage as a spiritual and intellectual friendship between husband and wife. This issue is also to be seen in a larger cultural context, as an ideal of modernity.[34]

In addition, it is characteristic of Aśk's dramatic style that his figure conception is psychological. Similar to the personages in naturalistic dramas, his characters possess a reduced level of awareness. They cannot see themselves from without. Thus, they perform their actions without being able to observe and discuss themselves at the same time. One noteworthy exception is found in the drama *Chaṭhā beṭā* (*The Sixth Son*). The employment of a transpsychological figure conception relates Aśk's play to Arthur Miller's *Death of a Salesman*. In both dramas, the action is partially replaced by memory scenes. Thus, in Miller's play, the protagonist is constantly afflicted by the memory of things that have happened in the past, which he experiences and lives out anew in his mind, simultaneously with the other actions he is performing at a particular moment. This occurs no

---

[31] ——, *Kaid aur uṛān* (Ilāhābād: Nīlābh, 1972) 44-5.

[32] ——, *Añjo Dīdī: do aṅkoṃ kā ek sāmājik nāṭak* (Ilāhābād: Nīlābh, 1983) 83-4.

[33] ——, *Svarg kī jhalak* (Ilāhābād: Nīlābh, 1971) 26-7.

[34] The dramatist has also reflected on this subject matter in the drama *Alag alag rāste*. While Madan's marriage with Sudarśan is shown to be immoral because of the unfair treatment of Rāj, the union of the two fellow students represents a spiritual and intellectual friendship between two partners. J. Māthur has discussed the nature of marriage along similar lines in his play *Rīṛh kī haḍḍī* (*Backbone*), 1939.

matter whether he is driving in his car or conversing with his son Biff or with his friend Charley. Miller's approach of merging past and present, of exposing the "inside of Willy's head" reminds one of cinematographic flashback technique. These simultaneous scenes enable the author to evoke a vision. They mark the dramatist's departure from the dramaturgy of naturalistic theatre, which aims at creating the illusion of photographic representation of reality. On the level of figure conception, Miller's method involves the employment of transpsychological elements. In this sense, Willy's constant memory visions represent unusual state of mind and partial loss of self, resulting in an increased degree of awareness.

Similarly, in the play *Chaṭhā beṭā*, Aśk makes the father, the drunkard Paṇḍit Basantlāl, dream in his sleep. He dreams that he has won a fabulous amount of money from the lottery. This fact changes his sons' attitude toward him completely. In the first scene, they complain about his misdeeds in their childhood and are ashamed of him. They do not even want him to stay in their house any longer, as this would ruin their reputations. In subsequent scenes, they are affectionate, respectful and obedient. The action in these scenes is presented as reality. It is performed on stage in front of the audience. The second scene shows a man sleeping on a bed and a lottery ticket lying beside him on the ground. This is the only fact that reveals the existence of a second action sequence. The presence of this additional built-up scenery on stage throughout the entire play, parallel to the other events, suggests the simultaneity of the two actions.

All the events happening in the third, fourth and fifth scenes of the play turn out to be just a dream in the end. This stylistic device enables Aśk to endow his protagonist with an exceptional level of self-awareness. Thus, through the way he envisions himself and his relation with his family after winning from the lottery, it becomes clear that the father is aware of the fact that he drinks heavily, that he has treated his wife badly and that his sons would love and respect him, and even tolerate and encourage his excessive drinking, if only he had money to give them.

Whereas Miller experimented with merging past and present, i.e. present action and memory-visions, Aśk merges present and future, i.e. present action and dream visions of a more affluent future. This similarity of dramaturgical approach, which manifests itself in the employment of transpsychological figure conception, is to be explained by the fact that there is also similarity in theme between the two plays. Thus, both dramas deal with the difficult relationship between father and sons, presenting the family not as a happy and blissful unit, but as a battleground charged with conflicts.[35] In addition, both playwrights handle the subject matter from an autobiographical perspective.

Characterization Techniques

Characterization is a suprahistorical category and refers to the formal techniques of information transmission that are employed to present a dramatic figure. Drama criticism distinguishes between figural characterization, if the information about a character is conveyed by one of the figures, and authorial characterization, if it is the author himself or the implied author who provides it.[36] As already discussed in the previous subdivision, the information could be sent explicitly or implicitly.

Two instances of explicit figural characterization technique are self-commentary and commentary by others. Though this technique is not widely used by Aśk, it does occur in several cases. Thus, in *Kaid*, Prāṇnāth's reminiscence of the past is a self-commentary.[37] In it he questions the moral aspect of his behavior when he agreed to marry Appī, who did not love him, and take her away from her home to far-off Akhnur. Similarly, in the last scene of *Añjo Dīdī*, Indranārāyaṇ explains in a self-commentary why he will not drink, even after he has come to know the real reason for his wife's death.[38] His self-commentary reveals him to be a loving and respectful husband, with a feeling for propriety, and makes clear to the audience that he is completely different from Śrīpat.

---

[35] At the center of Miller's play, is the issue of the American dream and the tragedy of the common man. In addition, the author also handles the questions of family life and the conflict between father and sons.

[36] See M. Pfister, *Das Drama. Theorie und Analyse* (Muenchen: Wilhelm Fink Verlag, 1988) 250.

[37] U. Aśk, *Kaid aur uṛān* (Ilāhābād: Nīlābh, 1972) 44.

[38] ——, *Añjo Dīdī: do aṅkoṃ kā ek sāmājik nāṭak* (Ilāhābād: Nīlābh, 1983) 110-1.

Also Raghu's self-commentary in the last scene in *Svarg kī jhalak* is a key to understanding his motives for not marrying Umā.[39] His utterance enables us to perceive him as a young man who is afraid of fighting for his happiness and who is unwilling to sacrifice his comfort. Māyā's self-commentary at the end of *Uṛān* makes clear to the three men around her that she wants an equal relationship, and could therefore accept none of them as her friend and future partner.[40] Her utterance characterizes her as an independent woman who knows what she wants in life, and who will fight for her dreams. In *Alag alag rāste*, there are several instances of explicit figural characterization technique through self-commentary. Thus, Tārācand's self-commentary on the reasons for Trilok's false expectations about the dowry reveals him to be a conservative man who sticks to the old rules and believes in the marriage customs of traditional Hindu society that are exploitive to women. Rāj's self-commentary on her relationship with her husband characterizes her as a loving woman capable of devotion and sacrifice. It shows that she was not blind to her husband's neglect, but was not willing to give him up before she has done her best to win his love.[41]

All the above-mentioned cases represent self-commentaries in the form of a dialogue. Pratibhā's utterance in the last scene in *Bhaṃvar* is one of the few instances of a self-commentary in the form of a soliloquy.[42] It reveals the heroine's troubled state of mind and poses one of the main questions of her dilemma: has she been obsessed with Nīlābh because she loves him or because she is running after the moon she can never have.

Sometimes the figures are characterized explicitly by commentaries from others. Thus, the servants' remarks on Appī's "imprisonment" in the drama *Kaid*, and Rānī's comment on the moral implications of Madan's behavior toward his wife, or Tārācand's commentaries on Madan's and Trilok's characters in the play *Alag alag rāste*, are instances where Aśk employs explicit figural characterization in the form of commentary by others to delineate his figures.[43]

---

39 ——, *Svarg kī jhalak* (Ilāhābād: Nīlābh, 1971) 104.

40 ——, *Kaid aur uṛān* (Ilāhābād: Nīlābh, 1972) 152.

41 ——, *Alag alag rāste* (Ilāhābād: Nīlābh, 1986) 64-5. 76.

42 ——, *Bhaṃvar* (Ilāhābād: Nīlābh, 1961) 11-2.

43 ——, *Kaid aur uṛān* (Ilāhābād: Nīlābh, 1972) 68; ——, *Alag alag rāste* (Ilāhābād: Nīlābh, 1986) 77. 81. 64-5.

Most often, Aśk portrays his figures by using verbal implicit figural characterization techniques. Whereas non-verbal implicit figural techniques of characterization refer to the physiognomy and facial expression, stature and gesture, masks and costume, or locale and behavior, verbal techniques are revealed in the choice of verbal behavior (idiolect, sociolect, register and stylistic texture of the utterances).[44]

Explicit authorial techniques of characterization refer to the authorial descriptions in the secondary text and the use of telling names.[45] Aśk provides abundant information about his figures' physical appearance, social and biographical background in order to portray his characters convincingly and realistically.

A playwright can also characterize the dramatic figures implicitly, by employing the stylistic device of correspondence and contrast, and by the choice of implicitly characterizing names.[46] Thus, Aśk presents the correspondences and contrasts between the figures to delineate their characters. These differences are often articulated by the figures themselves. In the second act in *Alag alag rāste*, the author makes Pūran and Trilok confront each other and engage in an intensive discussion about the values of life, marriage and tradition. Both protagonists express their views openly and it is not difficult to define Pūran as an honest and educated young man of progressive opinion, and an advocate of women's rights. We are aware of the fact that the author sympathizes with him. Conversely, Trilok is portrayed as a conservative person who believes in a society dominated by masculine authority; he does not love his wife but is interested in her only because of the profit she could bring him.[47] Consequently, by employing this technique, the author enables the audience, who is the receiver of the information, to make contrasting comparisons and to form its opinion of the figures' characters by itself.

Another instance of emphasis on the stylistic device of contrast and correspondence is the dialogue between husband and wife in the one act

---

[44] See M. Pfister, *Das Drama. Theorie und Analyse* (Muenchen: Wilhelm Fink Verlag, 1988) 257-61.

[45] ibid. 62. In Aśk's plays, there are no instances of implicit authorial characterization by means of employment of telling names.

[46] ibid. 263-4.

[47] U. Aśk, *Alag alag rāste* (Ilāhābād: Nīlābh, 1986) 91-107.

play *Taulie*. In the stormy disputes about how to use the towels at home, Madhu and Vasant reveal the contrasting features of their characters. We come to know about their different social background and upbringing, and the different expectations they have brought with them into their marriage. While Madhu was brought up in a luxurious home, Vasant grew up in a family where there was not enough money and family members could not afford individual towels. However, despite the poverty, the husband spent his childhood in a home where there was a lot of warmth and people were close to each other. His wife, on the other hand, grew up in a sterile but cold atmosphere, where cleanliness was used as an excuse for not being able to come into physical contact with the others.[48] By making Madhu and Vasant articulate their contrasting viewpoints, the dramatist implies that husband and wife are both right and wrong in blaming the other, and that the only solution is to be tolerant and make compromises.

An additional possibility of characterizing the personages by emphasizing contrasts and correspondences between them is to confront several figures with a similar situation simultaneously or consecutively, and thus establish their individuality by comparing the different ways in which they react to it. For instance, in *Alag alag rāste*, Aśk confronts both Rānī and Rāj with a similar situation. Both women were unhappy at home and have left their husbands, seeking refuge and protection in their father's house. In the end, it is possible for both of them to go back. But whereas Rānī refuses to return to her husband and decides to start a new life, Rāj accepts humiliation and goes back to Madan and his new wife. By showing the similarity in their situations and the different ways in which they react, Aśk underlines their individuality.

An author can characterize the figures through contrasts by pointing out the different ways in which they address another figure or theme. Thus, in *Uṛān*, Śaṅkar, Rameś and Madan are characterized by their different attitudes toward Māyā. Whereas Śaṅkar wants to destroy and "conquer" her, Rameś worships her devotedly, and Madan cares about her only as long as he feels that he can possess and control her.

The contrasting way in which Appī's relationships to Prāṇnāth and to Dilīp are presented serves to characterize the heroine. In the presence of her

[48] ——, "Taulie," *Paccīs śreṣṭh ekāṅkī* (Ilāhābād: Nīlābh, 1969) 79-103.

husband, she is apathetic and ill, and does not feel like joining him for a walk. Only the news of her friend's arrival makes her lively, energetic and full of hope. She not only goes for a walk with him, but also enjoys it and admires the beauty of the place she has only detested so far. In this way, it is clear to the audience that she loves Dilīp, and not Prāṇnāth, and that the real reason for her illness is her unhappy marriage. The examples discussed show that figure delineation on the basis of correspondence and contrast between the figures is one of the implicit characterization techniques most widely employed by Aśk.

Another instance of implicit authorial characterization is the use of interpretative names, enabling the audience to associate a dramatic figure with a particular feature of its character. This stylistic device is important in drama, where the absence of mediating communication system limits the possibilities of transmitting information and of characterizing by means of additional narrative elements. Thus, it is no coincidence that Rāj's and Rānī's names mean "kingdom" and "queen," Pratibhā's "genius, brilliance," Māyā's "illusion" and Appī's (Aparājitā's) "unconquered."

Both Rāj and Rānī appear to be queen-like in their behavior, living up to all their ideals with much devotion and sacrifice, Rāj by following the primordial way, and Rānī, by venturing to go along a new path in life. Pratibhā's intellectualism and exceptional ability to think and reflect upon her fate is also revealed in the choice of her name. Māyā turns out to be like an illusion for the three men that feel attracted by her. On another level, the choice of her name may point to the fact that she is not to be found in real life. There are few women who are as emancipated and tenacious in the pursuit of happiness as she is. Similarly, Appī's name symbolizes her love for Dilīp that can be "conquered" neither by her husband nor by the power of time. In this sense, the use of interpretative names for the main protagonists enables the dramatist to enrich their characters by suggesting additional possibilities of interpretation.

Chapter Four

Story and Plot. Time and Space

Story and Plot

The concept of story refers to the totality of interlinked events reported in a dramatic text. The term "plot" alludes to the same events but in their representation, in the order in which they are communicated in the work. Thus, the distinction between "story" and "plot" in modern drama criticism corresponds to that made by Russian formalists with reference to the use of "sujet" and "fable."[1] We shall therefore proceed to explore how Aśk presents the story, i.e. the techniques of story presentation he employs. As regards the question of plot, we shall study the segmentation of the different events and actions[2] and the peculiarities of composition.

---

[1] See M. Pfister, *Das Drama. Theorie und Analyse* (Muenchen: Wilhelm Fink Verlag, 1988) 266-8.

[2] The term "story," in German "Geschichte," can also be defined as a sequence of actions, a chain of events or a combination of the two. The concept of action refers both to a single action by a particular figure in a given situation and to the overall action of the whole text, in German "Handlung" and "Handlungssequenz." The term "action" in its first meaning, as

Techniques of Story Presentation

A story can be presented either directly in scenic form, or can be mediated narratively in the figures' speeches. For the scenic presentation, the principle of succession applies. This means that the scenic presentation follows strictly the order of actions and events as they happen in the story. Overlaps in the actions do not occur if the dramatist involves different sets of figures for different action sequences. The principle of succession makes impossible the use of flashback techniques, which are widely used in narrative texts and film. This restricts the possibility of presenting simultaneous actions and events. Only those that take place within the same locale can be presented simultaneously. The violation of the succession principle reveals a tendency to create epic structures or establish a mediating communication system, similar to that characteristic of narrative texts.

The story can be mediated narratively either in the form of a messenger's report or in the figures' speeches, in the form of narratively mediated background information about previous events.[3] These devices of narrative mediation allow the dramatist to reproduce in a condensed form action sequences that belong to the story and inform the audience, but are not being presented scenically.

A question arises: how are the different action sequences, on which the plot is based, coordinated in the dramatic text?[4] Two or more functionally equal sequences, that is two or more "plots," can be either juxtaposed or

---

opposed to the term "event," in German "Geschehen," connotes the intentionally chosen transition from one situation to the next. The term "event" implies that either the human subjects are incapable of making a deliberate choice or that the situation does not allow any change (ibid. 268-73).

[3] The technique of teichoscopy, used mainly in classical Greek drama, is another instance of narrative mediation. An off-stage action, for instance a battle, which is simultaneously taking place with the action on stage, is communicated to the audience in the form of reportage. Whereas the messenger's report refers to events that have already happened and need to be integrated into the main plot, the teichoscopy relates to simultaneous actions and aims at increasing the dramatic suspense. Aśk does not employ this technique in his plays.

[4] Modern drama criticism does not adhere to the Aristotelian notion of the "unity of plot" that postulates that the plot should be based only on one single action sequence. See M. Pfister, *Das Drama. Theorie und Analyse* (Muenchen: Wilhelm Fink Verlag, 1988) 285.

strung together successively. It is also possible to coordinate the sequences on a hierarchic pattern. In this way, one of the plots is enlarged by one or more "subplots."[5]

We should ask next whether the interconnected action sequences are connected on the same fictional (dramatic) level or whether they are superimposed on one another on different levels. Coordination techniques like the dream inset and the play-within-the-play are instances where a primary dramatic level contains within itself a secondary dramatic level.[6] By using such epic structures, the dramatist aims at involving the audience in the play and destroying dramatic illusion.

The principle of succession and the possibility of presenting simultaneous events, taking place within the same locale by involving different sets of figures, can be illustrated in the example of the drama *Alag alag rāste*. Thus, although the conversations both between Tārācand and his friends, and between Rānī and Rāj occur simultaneously, the two action sequences can be presented successively on stage without any overlapping, as the personages are different and the locale is the same.

Instances of narrative presentation in Aśk's plays are numerous. Most often, background information is transmitted narratively, in the figures' utterances. Thus, we learn about all the events prior to the opening scene of the drama *Kaid*, through Prāṇnāth's conversation with his wife. His reminiscences about the past are highly informative for the audience.[7] We learn about his wife's death, the circumstances under which he married his second wife, and what she and her life were like before meeting him. All this information helps us to grasp the current situation presented scenically on stage, and to see the reasons for Appī's illness and unhappiness. Similarly, in *Svarg kī jhalak*, the audience becomes acquainted with facts about Raghu's first marriage through Raghu's semi-monological remarks on the subject. The information about the quarrels with his wife, who was uneducated and did not understand him, is transmitted narratively, in Raghu's conversation with his brother.[8] Another instance of narrative mediation presents the second act of the drama *Añjo Dīdī*. Thus, we learn

---

[5] ibid. 286-90.

[6] ibid. 290-307.

[7] U. Aśk, *Kaid aur uṛān* (Ilāhābād: Nīlābh, 1972) 44-5.

[8] ——, *Svarg kī jhalak* (Ilāhābād: Nīlābh, 1971) 26-7.

about Añjo's death and the events occuring in the past twenty years from Omī's words, addressed to Animā.[9] Also in the play *Uṛān*, the background information about Māyā's flight from the bombing in Burma and the loss of Madan is mediated narratively. She reports these events when she meets Śaṅkar and Rameś.[10] Similarly, in *Alag alag rāste*, Rāj's narration of her relationship with her husband informs not only Rānī, but also the audience, of the true nature of her marriage and Madan's character. In this sense, Tārācand's conversation with his friends is highly informative as well. In it, the author presents the story of Rānī's marital life and the past events that caused the problems and later on led to her flight from her husband.[11]

In the drama *Alag alag rāste*, Aśk has employed another technique of narrative mediation, namely a messenger's report. Thus, at the end of the first act, Śivrām appears and announces that Tārācand's son-in-law is getting married for the second time. The audience realizes immediately that it is Madan, and not Trilok, who is getting married, as it has already received advance information through Rāj's narration. Tārācand, however, is genuinely surprised. The dramatic irony created by the author aims at increasing the dramatic suspense. Thus, the employment of techniques of narrative mediation enables Aśk to present simultaneous actions or background information, essential both to the delineation of the characters and to the further development of the conflict in condensed form.

A survey of the majority of Aśk's plays shows that most common aspect of his dramatic style is the use of hierarchic patterns of coordination of the action sequences. His dramas consist of one main plot that is complemented and complicated by the existence of many subplots. Let us illustrate this point by looking closely at the play *Alag alag rāste*. The main plot refers to conversations between Tārācand and his friends, the news of Madan's second marriage in the first act, and, in the third act, Tāracand's return home. His arrival is marked by his failure to prevent the marriage and by his confrontation with his daughter Rānī who disobeys him and leaves his home. Many subplots are connected to this main plot, as revealed in Rāj's and Rānī's conversation, in Pūran's and Trilok's encounter, in the meeting between Trilok and Rānī, and in Udayśaṅkar's conversation with Rāj. These

9 —, *Añjo Dīdī: do aṅkoṃ kā ek sāmājik nāṭak* (Ilāhābād: Nīlābh, 1983) 69-70.

10 —, *Kaid aur uṛān* (Ilāhābād: Nīlābh, 1972) 113-4. 136-8.

11 —, *Alag alag rāste* (Ilāhābād: Nīlābh, 1986) 60-5. 73-8.

subplots reveal the real state of affairs, including the two women's marriages, the parents' responsibility for the unhappiness of the young people, and the immoral character of both Madan and Trilok.

The insertion of subplots, such as the ideological dispute between Trilok and Pūran or the emotionality of the scene in which Udayśaṅkar entreats Rāj to return home and accept Madan's co-wife in order to save the good name of the family, broaden the dimension of the conflict. The action is no longer related only to Rānī's and Rāj's individual fates. The author points to the commonality of the problems discussed and shows clearly the conflict between tradition and modernity: should a woman submit to tradition, the "primordial way," as Rāj does, or should she accept the uncertainty and difficulties of the new way, similar to Rānī.

Though most of Aśk's plays are influenced by naturalistic dramaturgy, which aims at creating the illusion of reality on stage, the author also experiments with new forms. He attempts to deliberately destroy the illusory character of his plays by employing epic structures. He achieves this by superimposing action sequences on different fictional levels, for instance through the insertion of a dream inset and a fictional play within the actual play.

Thus, in the play *Chaṭhā beṭā*, the primary dramatic level contains within itself a secondary fictional level. The primary dramatic level is presented in the first and in the fifth scene. The scenes in-between are informed by Paṇḍit Basantlāl's dream. The dream sequences are staged multimedially and the stage is transformed into the inner chambers of the dreamers's mind. Aśk visualizes the simultaneity of the two action sequences by staging both of them, dividing the stage into two parts. In the illuminated one, the dream sequences are performed as if they were really happening. In the dimly illuminated part of the stage, the audience sees a bed and a man sleeping on it. A lottery ticket is lying on the floor. Until the final utterance of the last scene, when the man wakes up and asks himself whether he has dreamt all this,[12] we are not aware of the superimposition of the two fictional levels. In this sense, Aśk employs the dream inset as an anti-realist technique, weakening the restrictions imposed by the dramatic medium on the presentation of inner psychic processes.

---

[12] ——, "Chaṭhā beṭā," *Ādi mārg: cār sāmājik nāṭakoṃ ke raṅgmañc saṃskaraṇ*, by U. Aśk (Ilāhābād: Nīlābh, 1961) 263.

A further attempt to compensate for the absence of a mediating system in drama by employing epic structures is revealed in the plays *Nayā purānā* and *Pardā uṭhāo! Pardā girāo*. The secondary fictional level is created by the introduction of a metaplay within the primary play. In this way, theatre and drama become their own themes. In *Pardā uṭhāo! Pardā girāo*, the theatrical rehearsal and the performance itself are the subject of the play. Aśk unmasks what he considers the bad conditions and the absence of professionalism of modern Hindi theatre. The actors either do not appear or are badly prepared. The performance itself is shown to be a fiasco.

It is interesting to note that the author also questions the nature of the relationship between real audience and real performance in this play. Thus, in the metaplay, the dramatist makes the fictional spectators act as commentators. They laugh at the lack of professionalism of the actors and loudly comment on all the mistakes during the performance. In this sense, the fictional spectators play roles, too, fictional audience is present on stage. In this satirical comedy, Aśk not only experiments with new dramaturgical forms in order to create an anti-realist and anti-illusionist work, but also writes a play-within-the-play drama to draw our attention to the plight of modern Hindi theatre.

Whereas in *Pardā girāo! Pardā uṭhāo* the real audience is aware of the fact that it is involved in a secondary, additional fictional level of a metaplay, in *Nayā purānā* (*New and Old*), this fact remains hidden from us until the very end of the play. The audience, who has become involved in the story the author tells, finds out only in the final scene that the performance it was made to believe to be the real drama was just a rehearsal, a play within a play. The illusion of reality is interrupted by the introduction of a commentator figure. The stage director leaves the place from which he has quietly been observing the rehearsal and interrupts the performance. He starts a discussion with the author of the play about the nature of realism and tells him that he cannot accept the drama to be staged at his theatre, as it is not realistic.

Aśk visualizes the simultaneity of the two action sequences by presenting scenically the two sets of figures. While the lights illuminate the characters of the metaplay, the stage director, who is silently sitting and smoking a cigarette, remains present and visible on stage throughout the entire play. The situation changes at the end of the drama. All the lights move on to him and the actor in the main role, who turns out to be the author of the play. In this respect, it is interesting to note that the two fictional levels are also reflected and visualized in the two persons played by the main figure. Under the name Devcanda, the actor, who the audience sees, is Lilī's teacher, and under the name Gajendra, he is the author of the play. Thus, by creating a play-within-the-play drama, Aśk reflects on the poetological nature of his realistic dramaturgical mode, undermining the illusory character of modern drama.

A study of the quantitative relations between the super- and subordinate (i.e. of the additional, secondary fictional level) plot sequences in Aśk's work, as reflected in the example of the three plays discussed above, shows that the subordinate sequences are qualitatively and quantitatively superior to the primary sequences. Thus, the subordinate plot sequences of the dream inset and the metaplay occupy the entire scenic time. Actually, they constitute the dramas, whereas the superordinate plot sequences are reduced to a kind of frame for the subordinate action sequences. Aśk's experimentation with new dramaturgical forms, such as the introduction of epic structures to create both a mediating system and destroy the illusion of reality on stage, and the coordination of action sequences on different fictional levels, is innovative for modern Hindi drama. Western theatre, and especially A. Miller's *Death of a Salesman* and Thornton Wilder's *Our Town*, have influenced this experimental approach.

Structural Segmentation and Composition

The distinction between story and plot can be formulated in terms of the distinction between the story and the dramatic presentation of that story. The story refers to the deep structural level of the text, while the dramatic presentation alludes to its surface level. The segmentation of the story is based on individual actions, events and their sequences. The segmentation of the presentation of the story, i.e. the structural segmentation on the surface, refers to changes in figure configuration, interruptions in the chronological order and spatial continuity of the play, the introduction of intervals, and the division into scenes and acts.[13]

Structural Segmentation

The smallest units of segmentation of the dramatic presentation are indicated by partial changes in the configuration. For instance, in *Alag alag rāste*, different configuration sets are represented by Tārācand and his friends, by Rānī and Rāj, by Rānī, Rāj and Pūran, by Trilok and Pūran, by Rānī and Trilok, by Rāj and her father-in-law Udayśaṅkar. The changes from one configuration to another enable the dramatist not only to present simultaneous actions without any overlaps, but also to signal the segmentation of the story, i.e. the introduction of additional strands to the main plot as well as subplots. Whereas a total change of configuration implies the creation of a new plot or subplot in the play, a partial change in the set of figures only complicates the existing plots. Thus, the shift from the figure set of Tārācand and his friends to that of Rānī and Rāj marks the introduction of another subplot. Conversely, the arrival of a new friend of Tārācand, who joins the other guests of the old *paṇḍit* ("learned man, Sanskrit scholar"), or Pūran's appearance on stage in a configuration set with Rānī and Rāj, presents additional strands to the already existing plot and subplot. In this way, the dramatic presentation of the story is clearly segmented through the deliberate changes in configuration that Aśk makes.

In addition, the structural segmentation of the story is marked by interruptions in the chronological and spatial continuity of the action sequences. In all the plays discussed so far, Aśk shifts the emphasis to later phases by transferring the early phases of the story into concise expository narratives. This technique brings about changes in the chronological continuity of the action. In the dramas *Kaid aur uṛān*, *Alag alag rāste* and *Svarg kī jhalak*, the author interrupts the chronological order of the current action sequence from the immediate present to the past in order to communicate background information to the audience. In the play *Chaṭhā*

[13] M. Pfister, *Das Drama. Theorie und Analyse* (Muenchen: Wilhelm Fink Verlag, 1988) 307-18.

beṭā, the action is transposed, not into the past, but into the dream-like future of the sleeping Paṇḍit Basantlāl. The introduction of the dream inset in *Chaṭhā beṭā*, and of a metaplay in *Nayā purānā* and in *Pardā uṭhāo! Pardā girāo* also brings about an interruption in the spatial continuity of the plays. Thus, the action sequence is moved from the stage either to the inside of the dreamer's mind or to the fictional stage of the metaperformance.

Another possibility of marking changes in time and space in the story is to segment the dramatic presentation into easily perceivable scenes and acts. Thus, the second act of the drama *Añjo Dīdī* indicates that twenty years have elapsed from the beginning of the story. The segmentation into different acts in *Svarg kī jhalak* marks predominantly the change of locale. In the first act, Raghu is at home, in the second act, he is at the Aśoks, in the third one, he visits the Rājendras, and in the fourth and final act, he is first at the theatre and then again at home. In the dramas *Alag alag rāste* and *Kaid*, not the changes in time or space, but the progress of the action and the complication of the conflict through the introduction of new figures serve as a basis for the segmentation into acts. Thus, in *Kaid*, the second act marks the arrival of Dilīp, the fourth one, of Vāṇī and Dilīp's friends. Similarly, in *Alag alag rāste*, the news of Madan's second marriage gives a new direction to the action, indicating the end of the first act. The second act shows the complication of the action through Trilok's arrival. In the final act, the failure to prevent the marriage, Udayśaṅkar's appearance and Rāj's decision to go back to Madan make the action progress toward the final "catastrophe." In the plays *Bhaṃvar* and *Chaṭhā beṭā*, where there are no acts, the structural segmentation of the dramatic presentation is indicated by the division into scenes.[14]

Aśk also experiments with new dramaturgical techniques through the segmentation of the dramatic presentation. Thus, in the one act play *Taulie*, the stage directions indicate a change in time, not by a division in scenes, but by a "fade in fade out" technique. The lowering and lifting of the curtain visualizes the fact that two months have elapsed between the two action sequences.[15] Similarly, in the drama *Chaṭhā beṭā*, where two different

[14] The different scenes of the drama *Chaṭhā beṭā* are not numbered. The raising and the lowering of the curtain and the page layout of the printed text mark the intervals between scenes.

[15] U. Aśk, "Taulie," *Paccīs śreṣṭh ekāṅkī*, by U. Aśk (Ilāhābād: Nīlābh, 1969) 91.

fictional levels are staged simultaneously, the curtain is raised and lowered, not only to signal the intervals between the scenes, but also to separate the two levels. Thus, at the beginning of the second scene, the primary dramatic level of the sleeping Paṇḍit Basantlāl is presented. Immediately thereafter, the curtain is lowered again. When it is raised anew, it reveals the secondary fictional level of the dream inset.[16]

Composition

Gustav Freytag's theory of the nature of the dramatic work was influential in the 19th century and continues to be so to the present day. Freytag considered the dramatic text to be based on a pyramid-like structure in which he discerned the following elements: introduction, rising moment, climax, fall, and catastrophe.[17] His ideas were a critical reflection on the historical dramatic form characteristic of the second half of the 19th century. The development of the dramatic genre in the subsequent decades no longer fitted into the narrow frames of Freytag's theory. In his influential work, Peter Szondi discussed the *Krise des Dramas* ("the crisis of drama") from the late 19th century onward and analysed its *Rettungsversuche* ("attempts at rescue") at the beginning of the 20th century, as well as the *Loesungsversuche* ("attempts at solution") by expressionist and experimental drama in the 1920s and 1930s.[18] Volker Klotz's study of the closed and open forms in modern drama examines the changes in composition that the new mode of dramatic writing brought about.[19] Thus, the ideal type of drama of the closed form corresponds to Freytag's model. Its characteristics are a self-contained story, in which there are no background events to influence the beginning, an absolutely final ending, and a linear, goal-oriented, and single-stranded plot whose presentation conforms to the Aristotelian demands of unity. Additional charactersistics

---

[16] ——, "Chaṭhā beṭā," *Ādi mārg: cār sāmājik nāṭakoṃ ke raṅgmañc saṃskaraṇ*, by U. Aśk (Ilāhābād: Nīlābh, 1961) 204-5.

[17] G. Freytag, *Die Technik des Dramas* (Leipzig: Hirzel, 1894).

[18] P. Szondi, *Theorie des modernen Dramas* (Frankfurt/M: Suhrkamp 27, 1970) 17-136.

[19] V. Klotz, *Geschlossene und offene Form im Drama* (Muenchen: Hanser, 1992).

are the use of language dominated by hypotactic syntax and figure conception that tends toward the portrayal of types.

With respect to Klotz's study, Aśk's dramas can be classified as dramas of the open form, in which there is no unity of plot. As discussed previously in this chapter, there is no linear plot in Aśk's plays. The author experiments with new forms, such as dream inset and the play-within-the-play dramatic model. Moreover, he employs other epic structures, such as introduction of commentator figures and inclusion of the audience in the performance. The main multi-stranded plot is complemented and complicated by subplots. The story is not self-contained and is influenced by the background events, mediated narratively in the figures' speeches. The author does not provide any solutions to the problems raised. The open-ended quality of his plays is another feature of open form drama.

Moreover, his figure conception is marked by individualization and psychologism, an additional deviation from the poetology of the closed form. However, Aśk's language reveals predominantly hypotactical structures, the utterances and dialogues are clearly constructed and there is no breakdown in communication. Therefore, Aśk's dramatic language has characteristics of closed form drama. Indeed, many modern dramas belong both to the types of the closed and open form, although one of the patterns predominates.[20]

In the following discussion, I will proceed to examine the composition in Aśk's plays. I will study the techniques of coordination of the different plot strands and the new structural patterns the author employs. Aśk coordinates the complementary strands of the plot by stringing them together successively. For instance, in the drama *Alag alag rāste*, the complementary subplots represented by the figure constellations of Rāni and Rāj, Rānī, Rāj and Pūran, Pūran and Trilok, Trilok and Rānī, and of Udayśaṅkar and Rāj are intertwined with the main plot represented by the figure constellation of Tārācand and his friends by the linking device of overlapping of actions and events. The simultaneity of the action sequences presented, the participation of all dramatis personae in the same events, and the relevance of the events

[20] Pfister broadens Klotz's model in his work. Thus, he does not aim at providing a theoretical model for the open form, but at identifying its different variants with regard to the story and its dramatic presentation. See M. Pfister, *Das Drama. Theorie und Analyse* (Muenchen: Wilhelm Fink Verlag, 1988) 320-7.

to all figures enable the author to coordinate the different complementary strands. The use of this coordination technique applies to almost all of Aśk's plays.

The drama *Bhaṃvar*, where the playwright employs the coordination technique of the central self, presents a single exception. In *Bhaṃvar*, the different plot strands are unified in the example of Pratibhā's figure. Every situation and all the additional characters of the play are designed in such a way as to shed light on her with all her physical, social and psychological characteristics. Unlike the central protagonist of closed form drama, the central self is the center of attention not because it initiates the most important actions, but because it is the object of that action. Thus, Pratibhā is the object of the actions of the male characters Hardatt, Jñāncand, Jagannāth and even of Nīlābh, who does not appear on stage. Through the introduction of these figures and through her reactions to their behavior, Aśk reveals her personality. She is characterized as an intelligent and refined woman who is unhappy because of her too romantic disposition and her love for an inaccessible man.

It is interesting to note that Pratibhā not only talks, but also thinks in the drama. The presentation of her thoughts intensifies the impression that she is the object of the others' actions. This coordination technique is innovative in the field of modern Hindi drama and Aśk is one of the first Hindi playwrights to employ it in his work. This is another instance of his creative encounter with Western theatre. Strindberg employed this device for the first time in his trilogy *To Damascus*, 1898–1904.

Aśk is influenced by Strindberg's dramaturgical method not only in the use of coordination techniques, but also in the composition of his plays. The open-ended quality of the plot is revealed in the choice of cyclical, repetitive structural patterns. Thus, in two of the dramas, in *Kaid* and in *Taulie*, the opening scene (the description of Appī's hopeless and apathetic human condition, and the quarrel of the married couple, respectively) is identical with the final one. The parallelism and repetition that marks the composition of these plays suggests that there is no solution to the conflict.

Whereas the open, unresolved ending in the play *Alag alag rāste* is still accommodated in the structural model of the closed form, beginning with an exposition (Tārācand's conversation with his friends), going through a climax (Madan's second marriage), and ending in a catastrophe (Rānī's flight into independence), the breakdown of linear finality in the plot in *Kaid* and in *Taulie* is given a new structural pattern.

Structures of Time and Space

Open and Closed Structures of Time and Space

Though Aristotle postulated only the unity of plot for the dramatic genre, in the 16th century, the theorists of drama also prescribed the unities of time and space as obligatory. This meant that dramatists were required to preserve a single locale throughout the entire drama and to equate the performance time with the fictional time-span of the play. The reception of Shakespeare's plays, in which the unities of time and space were not kept, and Lessing's ideas as revealed in *Hamburg Dramaturgy*, 1767, led to the abolition of the requirement of the unities of time and space as a norm in the 18th century.[21]

Similar to classical and classicizing dramas, most naturalistic dramas are based on self-contained and concentrated structures of time and space. However, the employment of closed structures of time and space does not bestow on them the character of closed dramas, as the conception of the figures, the making of dialogue and action are innovative, and their plot and composition are constructed in conformity with open form of drama. Thus, in naturalistic drama, there is sometimes discordance in the structures of time and space, the one being open and the other closed. In his study, Pfister illustrates this point by referring to Thornton Wilder's *The Long Christmas Dinner*, 1931, where the closed locale represented by the dining room of the Bayard family is set against an open time frame that encompasses ninety years of family history.[22]

Characteristic of Aśk's dramatic style, which is influenced by naturalistic dramaturgy and by Thornton Wilder's method, is that he employs mixed forms of space and time structures. Most often, if the

---

[21] ibid. 330-2.

[22] ibid. 338.

structure of space is open, that of time is closed and vice versa. Thus, in the dramas *Añjo Dīdī*, *Taulie*, *Bhaṃvar*, *Kaid* and *Alag alag rāste*, there are no changes of locale, but the fictional time of the story does not coincide with the real time of the performance. The action of all four plays is set within the limits of Añjo's, Madhu's, Appī's and Tārācand's homes respectively. In *Añjo Dīdī*, the fictional time exceeds the actual time of the performance with twenty years, as twenty years elapse between the first and the second act of the play. In *Taulie*, the interval of time between the two scenes is two months. In *Bhaṃvar*, there is a time lapse of an hour and a half between every scene. Besides, the scene depicting Pratibhā having coffee with her admirers at Connaught place is presented off-stage, thus extending the duration of the fictional time of the story. Similarly, in *Alag alag rāste* and in *Kaid*, there is discordance between fictional and actual time, too. For example, the scenes of Madan's second marriage and the old *paṇḍits*' attempt to prevent it in *Alag alag rāste*, and Dilīp's and Appī's walk in the third act of *Kaid* take place off-stage. Moreover, in the stage directions of *Kaid*, Aśk points to the fact that the second act plays one hour after the first one, and that there is a lapse of two hours between the successive two acts. Consequently, the duration of the fictional time of the story goes beyond the actual time of the performance.

Conversely, in the dramas *Chaṭhā beṭā*, *Nayā purānā*, *Pardā uṭhāo! Pardā girāo* and *Svarg kī jhalak*, the locale changes, whereas fictional and actual time coincide. In *Chaṭhā beṭā*, the space is divided into two. Throughout the whole play, two locales are presented scenically, the one shows the sleeping father on stage and the other serves as the space where the scenes of his dreams take place. Similarly, in *Nayā purānā* and in *Pardā girāo! Pardā uṭhāo*, there are two locales, the fictional stage of the performance and the actual stage of the play. In *Svarg kī jhalak*, the locale changes in every act, and is represented by Raghu's, the Aśoks', the Rājendra's homes and the theatre hall respectively. In all four plays, Aśk employs closed structures of time and there is no discordance between the fictional time of the story and the actual time of the performance.

Functions of the Structures of Time and Space

An important feature of naturalistic drama is the replacement of the public locale of classical drama by the private interior of a modern house. This spatial approximation of the fictional locale to the real world of the audience results from the author's intention of exposing the evils of his immediate environment. An additional characteristic of naturalistic dramaturgy is the description of the locale in detailed stage directions. The interior of the house, the figures' appearance and costume are depicted as extensively and precisely as in a narrative text. This approach serves to recreate the illusion of reality on stage. Moreover, the detailed descriptions of the material surroundings have the additional function of showing the extent to which the figures are conditioned by external circumstances and their social milieu.

It is characteristic of Aśk's dramatic style that he depicts the stage-set with epic thoroughness. In all the plays discussed in this chapter, the stage directions encompass two to four pages in which the figures' surroundings are described to the minutest detail. Thus, in *Kaid*, the author portrays the exterior and the messy interior of Appī's house in such a precise way that we even learn that the protagonist's bed sheets are dirty.[23] The detailed stage directions contribute to the recreation of the illusion of reality on stage. In addition, the chaos and untidiness of the interior of the house, which contrast with the splendor of the exterior, suggest Appī's social circumstances. Although she lives in a rich and beautiful house, she is unhappy and apathetic. Thus, her bed sheets are of silk but dirty. This contrast is intensified in the stage directions to the second act, where the same room is totally transformed. The young woman, who is looking forward to Dilīp's arrival, has become lively and energetic. The changed interior of her house, which is now clean and tidy, reflects her happiness and joy.

Similarly, in the drama *Añjo Dīdī*, the stage directions describe not just the wealthy house of a lawyer. The special attention Aśk gives to the clinical cleanliness of all things, which is the result not of the servants' but

[23] U. Aśk, *Kaid aur uṛān* (Ilāhābād: Nīlābh, 1972) 39.

of Añjo's efforts, serves to prepare the ground for the portrayal of Añjo's obsession with order and spotless cleanliness. The stage directions to the second act make it clear that little has changed in the past twenty years. The furniture is the same, but there is a five-year old calendar on the wall. The fact that Animā's style of dressing and wearing her hair are also of twenty years ago suggests not only the standstill in the entire house, but also in her personal life. Even before Aśk has explicitly stated it in the play, the audience guesses that Animā, who is forty-five years old now, has not married.[24]

Localization Techniques and the Presentation of Time

The examples discussed hitherto show that the playwright most often employs verbal and visual localization techniques. Thus, time and locale in the plays are explicitly defined in the stage directions, in the secondary text. Aśk states the color and the way the furniture is arranged, how many doors and chairs there are in the rooms, and whether it is ten o'clock in the morning or five o'clock in the afternoon. All these details are easily visualized during the stage performance, thus conveying exact information about the time and space structure of the play.

Besides, the playwright also uses non-verbal localization techniques. For instance, the exits and entrances of the dramatic figures serve to define the locale of the play. In the drama *Alag alag rāste*, the action sequences alternate between the entrances and exits of either Tārācand and his friends or Rānī and Rāj. Thus, the author suggests that the two simultaneous action sequences take place in two different rooms of Tārācand's house.

Another instance of the employment of non-verbal localization techniques are the announcements made by the dramatic figures in their utterances. In this respect, we are aware of the locale and time of Madan's second marriage through Śivrām's messenger's report.[25] This action is neither visualized on stage nor presented by the author in the secondary text. Similarly, the locale where Appī lives is defined in the servant's utterances.

[24] See U. Aśk, *Añjo Dīdī: do aṅkoṃ kā ek sāmājik nāṭak* (Ilāhābād: Nīlābh, 1983) 25. 65-6.
[25] ——, *Alag alag rāste* (Ilāhābād: Nīlābh, 1986) 82.

Kiśansinh states that she "got imprisoned in this desolate place,"[26] thus providing the audience with important information about the protagonist's surroundings.

The absolute autonomy of the dramatic genre, which Peter Szondi discusses in his book,[27] or the absence of a mediating narrator, presupposes the predominance of the present tense in drama. Despite the immediacy of the dramatic situation, the audience and the figures are aware of the past and future dimension of time. It is characteristic of Aśk's dramatic style that he relates the past to the present by introducing background events in the form of expository information that is mediated narratively, in the figures' utterances. Thus, the fictional time of the play *Kaid* does not start with the immediate conversation between Appī and Prāṇnāth presented on stage, but with that of eight years ago when they had first met in Delhi after the death of Appī's sister. Similarly, in *Alag alag rāste*, the past dimension is related to the present through Tārācand's expository narration of the pre-history of Rānī's conflict with her husband. In both dramas, these background events of the past are verbally related to the immediate current situation.

An additional characteristic of the presentation of time in Aśk's plays is that time is conceived as chronological progression and succession of events rather than a static condition. If we compare any of Aśk's dramas with Beckett's play *Waiting for Godot*, we can easily state that whereas in Aśk's plays things "happen," and the action and the conflict develop and progress, indeed toward an unresolved ending, in Beckett's play, time is seen simply as duration, as prolongation of a static condition: waiting for Godot. The chronological progression of time in Aśk's plays conveys the notion of future dimension of the action presented. The feeling of future expectancy is intensified by the open-ended quality of the author's dramatic method. The conflicts are left unresolved, the audience is aware of their further development in the future. Thus, in *Alag alag rāste*, time progresses to the point where Rānī will leave her father's house. However, the audience senses that time does not stop there and is aware of the future dimension of the action.

Though the plot is not linear in *Alag alag rāste*, the progression of time is linear. Time is conceived as starting in the past and heading for the future.

---

[26] ——, *Kaid aur uṛān* (Ilāhābād: Nīlābh, 1972) 98.

[27] P. Szondi, *Theorie des modernen Dramas* (Frankfurt/M: Suhrkamp 27, 1970) 13-5.

The linear progression of time is typical of the majority of Aśk's plays. In the dramas *Kaid* and *Taulie*, however, time progresses in a cyclical way. Although there is a certain idea of progression, the notion we get is that time starts from an initial point, moves through a number of other positions before returning to a point identical with the initial point. Thus, in *Taulie*, time starts from the point of the quarrel between Vasant and Madhu, moves through Madhu's being alone and meeting people in the two months of Vasant's absence and, at the end of the play, returns to a point in the future which is identical with the initial point of their quarrel in the past. Time does not progress in a linear but in a cyclical way.

Conclusion

This book acquainted us with the beginnings of modern Hindi theatre, the periodization and main tendencies in the development of Hindi theatre, and with selected works of six major Hindi playwrights. Further, we focused on the life and literary biography, dramatic work and dramatic style of one representative playwright, Upendranāth Aśk.

We discerned Prasād's neo-Sanskritic plays, Bhuvaneśvar's, Māthur's, Rākeś's and Aśk's pro-Western naturalistic dramas, and nativistic dramas after the 1960s. Whereas Prasād wrote in conformity with the aesthetic of classical Sanskrit drama and set the action of his historical plays in the great Hindu past, naturalistic Hindi playwrights created predominantly social problem dramas in which they concentrated on topical issues. Their plays were meant for the proscenium theatre and were influenced by the dramaturgy of Western drama. To Prasād's highly Sanskritized Hindi, they opposed a comprehensible Hindi and even a colloquial Urduized Hindustani. Thus, modern naturalistic Hindi drama originated and developed under the influence of Western dramatic tradition.

The historical context not only of Aśk's formation as a dramatist, but also of all the authors discussed after Prasād, draws on Western naturalistic dramatic tradition. L. Miśra set the beginnings of the creative encounter of modern Hindi drama with Western dramatic tradition. J. Māthur and Bhuvaneśvar continued writing naturalistic plays for the Hindi stage. Bhuvaneśvar's dramatic production is also one of the most powerful indigenous sources that inform Aśk's work as a playwright. For his admiration for the subject of the battle of the sexes, Aśk is indebted not only to Strindberg, but also to Bhuvaneśvar. In his work, Aśk develops further his predecessor's quest in the field of dramaturgical technique and dramatic language. Additionally, there are similarities in the interpretation of women's issues by J. Māthur and Aśk. In their employment of new dramatic forms, both authors are inspired by Western naturalistic theatre. Though M. Rākeś was more conservative and traditional in his portrayal of female characters than Aśk, both playwrights write in the wake of Western dramatic tradition.

The examination of Aśk's dramatic style shows the influence of Western naturalistic theatre. For the open-ended quality of the plays he is indebted to Ibsen, for the cyclical composition to Strindberg, for the psychological characterization to Chechov. The language of the dramatic figures serves to portray them in connection with their social background and individual circumstances. Although it can be defined as everyday Hindustani, it is interspersed with Punjabi, Braj, Urdu or English words for the purpose of characterization. The clearly discernible gender specific qualities of Aśk's dramatic language point to the importance of the issue of gender in the plays. The linguistic features of dialogue are typical of the closed dramatic form. The predominant syntactical structure of the sentences is marked by hypotaxis, and the temporal arrangement of the figures' utterances shows no disruption of communication.

Dramatic speech not only enables the figures to perform action on stage, but is also used as a means of characterization by the author. It enables him to compensate for the lack of narrative medium in drama. Most often, background information about the figures' past is transmitted narratively, in the form of informative expositions that are integrated in the utterances of the personages. Besides, the employment of epic techniques, such as the introduction of commentator figures, allows the dramatist to undermine the dramatic illusion of reality and explicitly communicate his ideas on specific subject matter.

Aśk's figure conception and characterization techniques are closely related to naturalistic dramaturgy, too. The dramatis personae are individuals whose characters and behavior are determined by their social milieu. It is characteristic of the author's dramatic style that he employs closed psychological figure conception. He provides extensive information about his characters and delineates them with reduced level of self-awareness. However, in the drama *Chaṭhā beṭā*, Ask experiments with new techniques of transpsychological figure conception. This innovative approach is a deviation from naturalistic theatre and is influenced by the expressionist technique in A. Miller's play *Death of a Salesman.*

Aśk employs both figural and authorial characterization techniques. As regards figural characterization techniques, the personages are portrayed explicitly, through self- and outside commentaries, or implicitly, through their physical, behavioral and verbal characteristics. Whereas the instances of explicit authorial characterization techniques in Aśk's plays refer to the descriptions in the secondary text, the figures are implicitly delineated by the choice of characterizing names and by the stylistic device of correspondence and contrast. It is also important to state the gender implications of the conception of character in Aśk's dramatic method. Thus, female characters are round and dynamic, and play a major role in the dramas, while male figures are of minor importance, and are often static and flat.

The treatment of story and plot in Aśk's plays reveals once again his proximity to naturalistic and experimental epic theatre. Thus, the playwright presents the story both directly, in scenic form, and narratively, in the figures' speeches. Narrative mediation through messenger's report and informative expositions enable the author to reproduce events not presented on stage in a condensed form.

The different action sequences are coordinated according to a hierarchic pattern. The main plot is complicated by the introduction of additional subplots. Aśk's innovative approach is revealed in the experimentation with the coordination of action sequences on different fictional levels. Arthur Miller's *Death of a Salesman* and Thornton Wilder's *Our Town* have influenced the insertion of a secondary fictional level, represented by a dream inset or metaplay, into the primary dramatic level. The nature of the plot, which is not linear, and the open-ended Ibsenite quality of Aśk's plays are characteristic of open form drama. The study of composition shows that the author employs new structural patterns of coordination of different plot strands. Thus, different subplots are linked not only by being strung together successively, but also by the coordination technique of the central self. This innovative coordination technique and the use of cyclical composition point to Strindberg's influence on the author's dramatic method.

The structures of time and space in Aśk's dramas reveal their proximity both to the dramaturgy of naturalistic theatre, where closed structures of time and space are used, and to Thornton Wilder's experimentation with mixed forms. It is characteristic of the playwright's dramatic style that he defines the circumstances of time and locale with epic thoroughness, as they serve not only to create the illusion of reality on stage, but also to provide details on the figures' social surroundings and personal behavior.

The author employs verbal and visual localization techniques. Thus, the stage directions contain extensive information about the stage-set, props and physical appearance of the figures. In addition, changes of locale are marked in a non-verbal way, through the entrances and exits of the figures, and through their announcements, in which there are references both to the time and space of the events presented. Time is conceived as linear chronological progression. Despite the immediacy of the dramatic situation presented, the audience is aware of the past and future dimensions of the action sequences through expository narratives of background events and through the open ending of the plays, in which the conflicts remain unresolved.

Let us now return to the question of influence and ideology in Aśk's dramatic work. Aśk is influenced by Western theatre and writes in the wake of Ibsen and Strindberg. Is he a naturalist? He writes socially committed literature and exposes the evils of society in his dramas. Is he a progressivist? My study showed that Aśk is one of the major Hindi playwrights. Then, why is he excluded from the literary canon of Hindi? Why does Hindi drama criticism ignore him and his work?

Aśk's literary biography was influenced by the socio-cultural climate and historical events of his time. The dramatist's social background, the influence of Indian progressivism and Western naturalistic theatre accounted for his realisitic and socially committed mode of writing. Aśk was affiliated closely both with the Indian Progressive Writers's Association and the Indian People's Theatre Association, and with the Parimal society, which was opposed to the dogmatism of the progressivist movement. The purposefulness and social commitment of the playwright's work bears witness to the progressivist message of his dramatic oeuvre. Thus, the author exposes social evils of Indian society and points to the oppression of women. He criticizes the existing social order in order to effect its reform. The peculiarities of his literary style, marked by experimentalism and innovative techniques, by an open-ended quality and a distanced tone, have prompted many of Aśk's contemporaries to overlook the progressivist ideal that underlies his literary production. Though this complexity of literary style accounts for the author's negative reception by

Indian critics to some extent, the main reasons for the exclusion of the dramatist from the canon of modern Hindi drama are ideological.

In the years after Independence, there was a strong resentment to Western ideas and cultural influence. Western dramatic school and naturalistic Hindi drama as its recipient were of crucial importance to the beginnings and further development of contemporary theatre in Hindi. However, the ideological apparatus of Indian criticism associated the notion of "Western" with the hegemonic position of the British in India. Because of political controversies with the British, "Western" influence also came to be understood as "non-Indian" in the sphere of literature. This resulted in a negative stance toward the naturalistic play of Hindi and those dramatists who adhered to it. Thus, the ideological discourse considered the neo-Sanskritic and the nativistic play of Hindi "Indian" in character, while the naturalistic play was discarded as pro-Western. Prasād's neo-Sanskritic plays were set as a standard, and naturalistic Hindi drama was looked upon as "non-Indian" or *videśī* ("foreign") in character.

This shift in ideology had a negative effect on the reception of the work of naturalistic playwrights, such as Aśk (and Bhuvaneśvar), who pronounced openly their admiration for Western dramatists. Aśk's dramatic achievement did not fit into the present-day critical discourse on modern Hindi drama. The reception of the author's dramatic oeuvre by contemporary Indian critics and his position in the Hindi world of letters was marked by neglect and exclusion from the canon. Whereas Mohan Rākeś and Jagdīścandra Māthur experimented with language, dramatic form and subject matter, and sought to borrow from classical Sanskrit theatre as well, Upendranāth Aśk was indisputably naturalistic and "pro-Western" dramatist.

The structuralist study of Aśk's dramatic style prompt me to make the statement that the dramatist's work should be considered a link between Western and modern Hindi drama. The innovative and experimental dramaturgical techniques reveal Aśk's creative encounter with Western tradition. Aśk is to be seen as innovator of modern Hindi theatre and as one of its most prominent representatives. Indian criticism today seeks to encourage a creative encounter of contemporary Indian theatre with classical Sanskrit drama or Indian folk theatre, not with Western naturalistic proscenium dramaturgy. The contoversial reception of Upendranāth Aśk's work by Indian drama criticism and the ensuing exclusion of the playwright from the literary canon of Hindi result from a general negative attitude toward the manifestation of Western cultural and theatrical influence in Hindi drama.

Bibliography

Primary Sources in Hindi

Aśk, Upendranāth. *Ādi mārg: cār sāmājik nāṭakoṃ kā raṅgmañc Saṃskaraṇ*. by U. Aśk. 1943. Ilāhābād: Nīlābh, 1961. 11-59.

——. *Alag alag rāste*. 1954. Ilāhābād: Nīlābh, 1986.

——. *Andhī galī: Nāṭak ke kṣetra meṃ ek nayā prayog*. Ilāhābād: Nīlābh, 1956.

——. *Añjo Dīdī: do aṅkoṃ kā ek sāmājik nāṭak*. 1955. Ilāhābād: Nīlābh, 1983.

——. *Āsmāṃ aur bhī haiṃ*. Ilāhābād: Nīlābh, 1973.

Aśk 75. Vol. 1. Nayī Dillī: Rādhākṛṣṇa, 1986. 2 vols.

——. *Baṛe khilāṛī*. 1967. Ilāhābād: Nīlābh, 1969.

——. *Bebāt kī bāt*. Dillī: Hindī Poket Buks, n.d.

——. *Bhaṃvar*. Ilāhābād: Nīlābh, 1961.

——. *Carvāhe*. 1948. Ilāhābād: Nīlābh, 1961.

——. *Cetan*. Ilāhābād: Nīlābh, 1952.

——. *Chaṭhā beṭā*. 1950. Ilāhābād: Nīlābh, 1971.

——. *Choṭī sī pahcān*. Ilāhābād: Nīlābh, 1971.

——. *Devtāoṃ kī chāyā meṃ*. Ilāhābād: Nīlābh, 1949.

——. *Girtī Dīvāreṃ*. 1967. Prayāg: Nīlābh, 1957.

——. *Jay parājay*. 1937. Ilāhābād: Nīlābh, 1984.

——. *Kaid aur uṛān*. 1950. Ilāhābād: Nīḷābh, 1972.

——. *Lauṭtā huā din*. 1972. Ilāhābād: Nīlābh, 1983.

——. *Mere priya ekāṅkī*. Ilāhābād: Racnā, 1975.

——. *Mere śreṣṭh raṅg ekāṅkī*. Nayī Dillī: Neśanal Pabliśiṅg Hāus, 1978.

——. *Mukhṛa Badal gayā*. Ilāhābād: Anāmikā, 1980.

——, ed. *Naye raṅg ekāṅkī: Sāt naye ekāṅkiyoṃ kā saṅgrah*. Ilāhābād: Nīlābh, 1956.

——. *Paccīs śreṣṭh ekāṅkī*. Ilāhābād: Nīlābh, 1969.

——. *Paiṃtre*. 1953. Ilāhābād: Nīlābh, 1967.

——. *Pardā uṭhāo! Pardā girāo*. 1951. Ilāhābād: Nīlābh, 1987.

——, ed. *Pratinidhi ekāṅkī*. 1950. Ilāhābād: Nīlābh, 1969.

——. *Rekhāeṃ aur citra*. Ilāhābād: Nīlābh, 1955.

——. *Sāhab ko zukām hai*. Ilāhābād: Nīlābh, 1959.

——, ed. *Saṅket*. Prayāg: Nīlābh, n.d. 109-84. 337-400.

——. *Svarg kī jhalak*. 1939. Ilāhābād: Nīlābh, 1971.

——. *Tūfān se pahle*. Ilāhābād: Nīlābh, 1972.

——. *Zyādā apnī: Kam parāyī*. Ilāhābād: Nīlābh, 1959. 207-16. 233-36.

Bedār, Rājeśvar, and Rājkumār Śarmā, ed. *Bhuvaneśvar Sāhitya*. Śahjahāṃpur: Bhuvaneśvar Prasād śodh sansthān, 1992.

Bhārtī, Dhamvīr. *Andhā yug*. 1954. Ilāhābād: Kitāb Mahal, 1967.

Hariścandra, Bhāratendu. *Andher nagarī*. 1881. Naī Dillī: Śārdā Prakāśan, 1978.

——. *Nīl Devī*. 1881. Dillī: Rājeś Prakāśan, 1977.

Māthur, Jagdīścandra. *Koṇārk*. 1951. Ilāhābād: Bhāratī Bhaṇḍār, 1961.

——. *Mere śreṣṭh raṅg ekāṅkī*. Dillī: Neśanal Pabliśiṅg Hāus, 1972.

——. *Bhor kā tārā*. 1937. Ilāhābād: Nīlābh, 1957.

——. *O mere sapne*. 1953. Ilāhābād: Nīlābh, 1960.

Miśra, Lakṣmīnārāyaṇ. *Rājyog*. Vārāṇasī: Sañjay Buk Senṭar, 1992.

——. *Sanyāsī*. 1929. Nayī Dillī: Vāṇī, 1993.

——. *Sindūr kī holī*. 1934. Ilāhābād: Bhārtī Bhaṇḍar, 2018 (vi.).

Prasād, Jayśaṅkar. *Candragupta*. 1931. Ilāhābād: Bhārtī Bhaṇḍār, 2017 (vi.).

——. *Dhruvasvāminī*. 1933. Ilāhābād: Bhārtī Bhaṇḍār, 2019 (vi.).

Prasād, Viśvanāth. *Lakṣmīnārāyaṇ Miśra racnāvalī*. Vol. 2. Vārāṇasī: Saṭjay Buk Senṭar, 1995. 2 Vols.

Rākeś, Mohan. *Ādhe adhūre*. 1969. Nayī Dillī: Rādhākṛṣṇa, 1985.

——. *Āṣāṛh kā ek din*. 1958. Dillī: Rājpāl eṇḍ sanz, 1963.

——. *Lahroṃ ke rājhaṃs*. 1963. Nayī Dillī: Rājkamal, 1990.

Siṃh, Śukdev. *Bhuvaneśvar kī racnāeṃ*. Vārāṇasī: Viśvavidyālay Prakāśan, 1976. 33-104.

Varmā, Rāmkumār. *Samāj ke svar*. Vol. 2. Dillī: Ātmārām eṇḍ sanz, 1982. 3 vols.

——. *Samāj ke svar*. Vol. 3. Dillī: Ātmārām eṇḍ sanz, 1984. 3 vols.

Primary Sources in English, German and Russian

Cechov, Anton P. *Polnoe sobranoe socinenij i pisem v 30 tomah*. Vols. 12-13. Moskva: Nauka, 1980. 30 vols.
The Collected Plays of Eugene O'Neill. London: Cape, 1988.
Ibsen, Henrik. *Four Major Plays*. Trans. Rolf Fjelde. Vol. 1. New York: The New American Library, 1965. 2 vols.
Miller, Arthur. *Collected Plays*. New York: Viking Press, 1967.
Shaw, Bernard. *The Complete Plays of Bernard Shaw*. London: Hamlyn, 1965.
Strindberg, August. *Dramen in drei Baenden*. Trans. Artur Bethke und Anne Strom. Ed. Arthur Bethke. Volumes 1-3. Muenchen: Carl Hanser Verlag, 1984. 3 vols.
Wilder, Thornton. *The Long Christmas Dinner and Other Plays*. New York: Harper, 1963.
——. *Our Town: A Play in Three Acts*. London: Longmans, 1959.
Williams, Tennessee. *Five Plays*. London: Secker, 1962.
——. *Four Plays*. London: Secker, 1968.

Reviews and Secondary Sources in Hindi

"Ādi mārg." *Kalpnā* August-October 1950: 183-4.
Agnihotrī, Śrīcandra. "Paiṃtre." *Rānī* December 1952: 65-6.
Agravāl, Premlatā. *Hindī nāṭakoṃ meṃ nāyikā kī parikalpnā*. Thāparnagar Meraṭh: Ramā Sāhitya, 1969.
"Alag alag rāste." *Ajantā* December 1955: 75-6.

Āḷekar, Mā.Bā. "'Jay parājay' nāṭak kī samīkṣā." *Jaybhāratī* January-February 1960: 9-13.

Aroṛā, Jñān. *Hindī sāhitya meṃ prahasan.* Naī Dillī: Ṭakṣaśilā, 1980. 160-74. 189-94.

Aśk, Kauśalyā, ed. *Aśk: Ek raṅgīn vyaktitva.* Ilāhābād: Nīlābh, 1961.

Aśk, Upendranāth. Prasaṅgvaś. *Lauṭtā huā din.* By U. Aśk. Ilāhābād: Nīlābh, 1972. 1983. 5-26.

—. "Hindī ekāṅkī aur jīvant raṅgmañc: Ek gahrī ḍhalān ke donoṃ chor." *Paccīs śreṣṭh ekāṅkī.* Ilāhābād: Nīlābh, 1969. 1-32ṇ.

—. "Hindī nāṭak-sāhitya par reḍiyo kā prabhāv." *Mādhyam* 9 (3): 53-6.

—. "Mere ekāṅkiyoṃ meṃ vyaṅgya kā srot." *Mukṛā badal gayā.* Ilāhābād: Anāmikā, 1980. 13-29.

—. "Nāṭakkār kī dṛṣṭi meṃ nārī." *Grāmyā* 25.5.1960: 5.

—. "Nāṭya-nirdeśak ko ek nāṭakkār kā uttar: Upendranāth Aśk." *Jñānoday* December 1963: 9-16. 179-83.

—. *Saṅket.* Prayāg: Nīlābh, n.d. 325-36.

Bajāj, Rāmpāl. "Aśk ke naye ekāṅkī." *Vīṇā* July 1953: 397-403.

"Baṛe khilāṛī." *Dharmyug* 27. April 1968: 45.

Benīpurī, Prabhā. *Benīpurījī ke nāṭakoṃ meṃ sāmājik cetnā.* Dillī: Kaipiṭal Pabliśiṅg Hāus, 1989. 83-90.

Bhāradvāj, Lakṣmīnārāyaṇ. *Raṅgmañc: Lokdharmī-nāṭyadharmī.* Indrāpurī: Ke. El. Pacaurī, 1992. 32-4. 114-22.

Bhāratī, Dharmvīr. Vyākhyā. *Kaid aur uṛān.* By U. Aśk. Ilāhābād: Nīlābh, 1972. 13-33.

Bhārgav, Bhāratratna. "Aśk: Apne hī mañc par." *Akath* June-July 1962: 67-73.

Bhārgav, Rāmeśvarnāth. *Hindī prahasan ke sau varṣ.* Dillī: Bhāvnā, 1980. 145-66.

Bhāṭī, Karṇa Siṃh. *Lakṣmīnārāyaṇ Miśra ke samasyā nāṭakoṃ kā svarūp viśleṣaṇ.* Nāgpur: Viśvabhāratī, 1981.

—. *Samasyā nāṭakkār Lakṣmī Nārāyaṇ Miśra.* Naī Dillī: Takṣaśilā, 1976.

Borā, Rājmal, and Nārāyaṇ Śarmā. *Hindī nāṭak aur raṅgmañc.* Jaypur: Pañcaśīl, 1988. 109-51.

Cātak, Govind. *Raṅgmañc: Kalā aur dṛṣṭi.* Naī Dillī: Takṣaśilā, 1988.

Dās, Mañjulā. *Prasādottar nāṭak meṃ rāṣṭrīya cetnā.* Dillī: Parāg, 1991. 100-69. 275-86.

Gauṛ, Añju Latā. *Hindī ekāṅkī meṃ jīvan-mūlya*. Meraṭh: Salabh, 1994. 241-360.

Gautam, Sureś, and Vīṇā Gautam. *Andhā yug kī racnā mānasiktā*. Naī Dillī: Śārdā, 1986.

Guptā, Kamal. *Aśk. Vyaktitva aur kṛtitva*. Jālandhar: Dīpak Pabliśarz, 1984.

Gupta, Paramlāl. *Āj kā hindī nāṭak aur raṅgmañc*. Ilāhābād: Naī Kahānī, 1997.

Gupta, Rāmkumār. *Hindī nāṭak ke pramukh hastākṣar*. Mathurā: Amar, 1980. 153-71.

Hemant, Nirmalā. *Ādhunik hindī nāṭyakāroṃ ke nāṭya-siddhānt*. Dillī: Akṣar, 1973. 235-404.

Jain, Nemicandra. *Ādhunik hindī nāṭak aur raṅgmañc*. Dillī: Maikmilan Kampanī, 1978. 120-34. 191-209.

——. "Ādhunik hindī nāṭak: Pratimān kā anveśaṇ." *Ālocnā* July-September 1967: 83-101.

——. *Janāntik*. Hāpuṛ: Saṃbhāvnā, 1981. 133-57.

——. "Mohan Rākeś kī nāṭya-bhāṣā." *Naṭraṅg* October-December 1972: 33-43.

——. "Nāṭak kā adhyayan." *Ājkal* April 1963: 15-30.

——. *Raṅg paramparā. Bhāratīya nāṭya meṃ nirantartā aur badlāv*. Nayī Dillī: Vāṇī, 1996.

Kālā, Mīnākṣī. *Prayogdharmī nāṭakkār Jagdīścandra Māthur*. Naī Dillī: Śārdā, 1983.

Kālṛā, Jīvanlatā. *Harikṛṣṇa 'Premī' ke nāṭakoṃ meṃ rāṣṭrīya bhāvnā*. Pañjāb viśvavidyālay kī em.e. (hindī) parīkṣā ke lie. Dillī: Sūrya, 1976.

Kamleśvar. "Añjo Dīdī: ek mūlyāṅkan." *Añjo Dīdī*. By U. Aśk. Ilāhābād: Nīlābh, 1983: 5-18.

Kathūriyā, Sundarlāl. *Prasādottar hindī nāṭak āsvād ke dharātal*. Dillī: Pāṇḍulipi, 1987. 101-35. 153-71.

——. *Prasādottar svātantrya-pūrva hindī nāṭak*. Dillī: Vikram, 1989. 110-28.

——. *Samkālīn hindī nāṭak*. Nayī Dillī: Paṅkaj Pustak Mandir, 1992. 33-47.

——. *Samsāmayik hindī nāṭak bahuāyāmī vyaktitva*. Dillī: Sāhityakār, 1979. 22-37.

Kumār, Rītā. *Svātantryottar hindī nāṭak: Mohan Rākeś ke viśeṣ sandarbh meṃ*. Bambaī: Vibhū, 1980. 13-48.

Kumār, Sudhīndra. *Hindī nāṭak. Paramparā aur prayog*. Dillī: Sañjay, 1998.
Kumār, Vacandev. *Hindī nāṭak: 1960 ke bād*. Paṭnā: Vibhū, 1982.
Kumār, Vinay. *Hindī ke samasyā nāṭak*. Ilāhābād: Nīlābh, 1968. 263-336.
Lāl, Lakṣmīnārāyaṇ. *Ādhunik hindī nāṭak aur raṅgmañc*. Ilāhābād: Sāhitya Bhavan, 1973.
Madān, Indranāth. *Hindī nāṭak aur raṅgmañc*. Dillī: Lipi, 1975. 40-95. 116-129.
——. *Upanyāskār Aśk*. Ilāhābād: Nīlābh, 1960.
Mahendra, Rāmcaraṇ. "'Aśk' ke sāmājik vyaṅgya." *Kalpnā* December 1951: 81-7.
——. *Ekāṅkī aur ekāṅkīkār*. Nayī Dillī: Vāṇī, 1989.
Mahto, Bhuvaneśvar. *Hindī ekāṅkī kā raṅgmañcīya anuśīlana*. Kānpur: Annapūrṇā, 1980. 165-270.
Malik, Śānti. *Hindī nāṭakoṃ kī śilpvidhi kā vikās*. Dillī: Neśanal Pabliśiṅg Hāus, 1971. 201-59. 327-446. 465-85.
Māthur, Jagdīścandra. *Nāṭakkār Aśk*. Ilāhābād: Nīlābh, 1954.
Miśra, Ānand Mādhav. "Hindī ekāṅkī sāhitya meṃ yathārthavād." *Nayā path* March 1955: 243-46.
Miśra, Satyaprakāś, ed. *Sṛjan aur parives*. Ilāhābād: Ilāhābād saṅgrahālay, 1997. 1-20.
Miśra, Sāvitrī, ed. *Pratijñā Pratīk. Upendra Nāth 'Aśk' par kendrit*. 11-12 (1998).
Miśra, Umeś Candra. *Lakṣmīnārāyaṇ Miśra ke nāṭak*. Ilāhābād: Hindī sāhitya Pres, 1959.
Miśra, Viśvanāth. *Hindī nāṭak par pāścātya prabhāv*. Ilāhābād: Lokbhāratī, 1966. 53-187. 269-409.
Ojhā, Daśrath. *Hindī nāṭak koś*. Dillī. Neśanal Pabliśiṅg Hāus, 1975.
——. *Hindī nāṭak: Udbhav aur vikās*. Dillī: Rājpāl eṇḍ sanz, 1995.
Ojhā, Māndhātā. *Hindī samasyā nāṭak*. Diss. Dillī U. Dillī: Neśanal Pabliśiṅg Hāus, 1968. 78-295.
Pālīvāl, Rītārānī. *Raṅgmañc. Nayā paridṛśya*. Naī Dillī: Lipi, 1980.
Paṇḍit, Vijay. *Raṅgmañc aur svādhīntā āndolan*. Nayī Dillī: Vāṇī, 1998.
Prasād, Jayśaṅkar. "Raṅgmañc." *Kāvya aur kalā tathā anya nibandh*. By J. Prasād. Ilāhābād: Bhārtī Bhaṇḍār, 2015 vi. 92-108.
Premlatā. *Ādhunik hindī nāṭak aur bhāṣā kī sṛjanśīltā*. Ilāhābād: Lokbhāratī, 1993. 98-205.

Raghuvaṃś. "Hindī ekāṅkī meṃ madhya-varg kī samasyā." *Ajantā* December 1955: 9-14.

Rājānanda. "Baṛe khilāṛī." *Vātāyan* March 1969: 63-4.

Rākeś, Mohan. *Sāhitya aur saṃskṛti*. Nayī Dillī: Rādhākṛṣṇa, 1990. 71-105.

Rastogī, Girīś. *Hindī nāṭak. Siddhānt aur vivecan*. Kānpur: Grantham, 1967. 279-340.

Rastogī, Sudhīndra. Bhūmikā. *Jay parājay*. By U. Aśk. Ilāhābād: Nīlābh, 1984. 10-40.

'Ratneś', Rāmāśray. *Hindī nāṭakoṃ meṃ naitik cetnā kā vikās*. Kānpur: Vidyā vihār, n.d. 255-71.

Rāy, Kapildev. *Sāhityakār Aśk*. Ilāhābād: Racnā, 1977.

Rāy, Lakṣmī. *Ādhunik hindī nāṭak. Caritra sṛṣṭi ke āyām*. 1979. Naī Dillī: Takṣaśilā, 1989. 142-78.

Rāy, Naranārāyaṇ. *Hindī nāṭak: Sandarbh aur prakṛti*. Dillī: Ke. El. Pacaurī, 1987. 9-32. 89-114.

——. *Jagdīścandra Māthur kī nāṭyasṛṣṭi*. Naī Dillī: Kādambarī, 1988.

——. *Nāṭaknāmā*. Dillī: Sanmārg, 1993. 47-49.

——. *Koṇārk. Raṅg aur saṃvednā*. Naī Dillī: Kādambarī, 1987.

Rāy, Tribhuvan, ed. *Nāṭakkār aur nāṭya samīkṣā*. Bambaī: Saṅkalp, 1982.

Śarmā, Jagdīś Datt, and Śyām Kiśor Śarmā. *Hindī ekāṅkī aur ekāṅkīkār*. Mujafaranagar: Prempurī, 1983. 57-63.

Śarmā, Jānkī Prasād. "Aśk pūrī Manzil par." *Samkālīn Bhāratīya Sāhitya* May-June 1998: 140-9.

Śarmā, Kiran Candra. *Hindī nāṭak meṃ vidroh kī paramparā*. Dillī: Vicār, 1991. 153-234.

Śarmā, M. L. *Ādhuniktā aur hindī ekāṅkī*. Dillī: Śabd aur śabd, n.d. 134-56.

Śarmā, Manoramā. *Udayśaṅkar Bhaṭṭ. Vyaktitva aur kṛtitva*. Naī Dillī: Ke. Bī. Pablikeśans, 1977.

Śarmā, Omprakāś. *Svātantryottar hindī raṅgmañc*. Kānpur: Atul, 1994. 106-96.

Śarmā, Rājkumār, ed. *Bhūvaneśvar. Vyaktitva evaṃ kṛtitva*. Lakhnaū: Uttar Prades Hindī saṃsthān, 1992.

Śarmā, Rāmjanma. *Svātantryottar hindī nāṭak 1947 se 1984 tak*. Ilāhābād: Lokbhāratī, 1985. 40-55. 67-78. 175-274.

Śarmā, Sūrajkānt. *Hindī nāṭak meṃ pātra-kalpnā aur caritra-citraṇ*. Dillī: Es. I. Es. Buk Kampanī, 1975. 196-216.

Śarmā, Śyām. *Ādhunik hindī nāṭakoṃ meṃ nāyak.* Naī Dillī: Abhinav, 1978.

Sāṭhe, Gajanan. "'Alag alag rāste' par..." *Rāṣṭravāṇī* January 1959: 53-60.

Siddhanāthkumār. *Hindī ekāṅkī kī śilp-vidhi kā vikās.* Dillī: Indraprastha, 1985. 201-11.

Siṃh, Es. Pi. "Aśk ke nāṭak aur ekāṅkī." *Ājkal* April 1966: 32-6.

Siṃh, Rām, and Śobhit Prasād. *Nāṭak samālocnā sandarbh.* Paṭnā: Jānakī, 1979.

Siṃh, Umāśaṅkar. *Hindī ke samasyā nāṭak.* Ilāhābād: Ūrjā, 1978. 108-61.

——. *Samasyā nāṭakkār Aśk.* Vārāṇasī: Sañjay Buk Senṭar, 1982.

Siṃh, Upendranārāyaṇ. *Ādhunik hindī nāṭakoṃ par aṅgla nāṭakoṃ kā prabhāv.* Dillī: Hindī sāhitya saṃsār, 1970. 172-221.

Sisaudhiyā, Malphāusiṃh. *Ādhunik hindī nāṭakoṃ meṃ nāyak evaṃ nāyikā kī parikalpnā.* Āgrā: Pragati, 1978. 333-342.

Sonvaṇe, Candrabhānu. *Dharmvīr Bhāratī kā sāhitya. Sṛjan ke vividh raṅg.* Jaypur: Pañcaśīl, 1979.

Śrīvāstav, Satīścandra. "Āñjo Dīdī: ek mūlyāṅkan. Aitihāsik paripārśav." *Āñjo Dīdī.* By U. Aśk. Ilāhābād: Nīlābh, 1983. 113-44.

Śukla, Sureścandra. *Ādhunik hindī nāṭak.* Naī Dillī: Lipi, 1981.

Sumanlatā. *Svātantryottar hindī aur telugu nāṭakoṃ meṃ nārī samasyāeṃ.* Masūrī: Ṛṣbhacaraṇ Jain evaṃ santati, 1988.

Surendrapāl. "Bhaṃvar. Ek vivecnātmak paricay." *Bhaṃvar.* By U. Aśk. Ilāhābād: Nīlābh, 1961. 9-48.

Sūryavaṃśī, Kamla. *Nāṭakkār Ḍa. Rāmkumār Varmā.* Diss. Marāṭhvāḍā Viśvavidyālay. Kānpur: Vikās, 1989.

Tanejā, Jaydev. *Āj ke hindī raṅg nāṭak. Pariveś aur paridṛśya.* Naī Dillī: Takṣaśilā, 1980. 9-114.

——. *Hindī raṅgkarm. Daśā aur diśā.* Naī Dillī: Takṣaśilā, 1993.

Tripāṭhī, Narendranāth. *Hindī nāṭak. Badalte āyām.* Dillī: Vikram, 1987. 55-101.

——. *Sāṭhottar hindī nāṭakoṃ meṃ strī-puruṣ sambandh.* Nayī Dillī: Sārasvat, 1985. 76-101.

Vāndiveḍkar, Candrakānt. "Alag alag rāste." *Rāṣṭravāṇī* June 1957: 51-3.

Varmā, Dineścandra. *Svātantryottar hindī nāṭak: Samasyāeṃ aur samādhān.* Kānpur: Anubhav, 1987. 9-50. 75-94.

Vārṣṇey, Raghuvardayāl. *Raṅgmañc kī bhūmikā aur hindī nāṭak.* Dillī: Vidyārthī, 1995.

Vātsyāyan, Saccidānand Hīrānand. "Jay parājay." *Viśāl Bhārat* December 1937: 719-20.
Vidyālaṅkār, Vidyāsāgar. "Baṛe khilaṛe." *Ājkal* January 1970: 44.
Vinay, ed. *Samkālīn hindī nāṭak aur raṅgmañc.* Dillī: Bhārtī Bhāṣā, 1981. 13-31.
Yādav, Rājendra. "Añjo Dīdī." *Jñānoday* January 1957: 94-6.
Yaqt, Aśok. "Upendranāth Aśk kī kāvya yātrā." *Gaganāñcal* 15 (1992): 30-42.

Secondary Sources in English, German and Russian

Asmuth, Bernard. *Einfuehrung in die Dramenanalyse.* 1980. Stuttgart: Metzler, 1994.
Bal, Mieke. *Narratology: Introduction to the Theory of Narrative.* Toronto: University of Toronto Press, 1985.
Berthold, Margot. *Weltgeschichte des Theaters.* Stuttgart: Alfred Kroener Verlag, 1968.
Borchmeyer, Dieter, and Viktor Zmegac, ed. *Moderne Literatur in Grundbegriffen.* Tuebingen: Niemeyer Verlag, 1994.
Buddruss, Georg. "Der Einakter 'Nayā purānā' von Upendranath Ashk." *STII* 2 (1976): 3-26.
—. "Zum Vorbild des Einakters 'Nayā purānā' von Upendranath Ashk." *STII* 7 (1981): 3-10.
Cossio, Cecilia. "Contradictions of the Feminine in the Writing of Mohan Rākeś." Ed. M. Offredi. *Literature, Language and the Media in India.* New Delhi: Manohar, 1992. 181-206.
Culler, Jonathan. *Structuralist Poetics: Structuralism, Linguistics and the Study of Literature.* London: Routledge & Kegan Paul, 1975.
Dalmia, Vasudha. *The Nationalization of Hindu Traditions: Bhāratendu Hariścandra and Nineteenth-century Banaras.* Delhi: Oxford University Press, 1997.
—. "A National Theatre for the Hindus: Hariścandra of Banaras and the Classical Traditions in Late Nineteenth Century India." Ed. M. Offredi.

Literature, Language and the Media in India. New Delhi: Manohar, 1992.

—. "Neither Half Nor Whole. Dialogue and Disjunction in the Plays of Mohan Rakesh." *Tender Ironies: A Tribute to Lothar Lutze.* Ed. Dilip Chitre et al. New Delhi: Manohar, 1994. 184-205.

Dimitrova, Diana. "The Indian Character of Modern Hindi Drama: Neo-Sanskritic, Pro-Western Naturalistic or Nativistic Dramas." Ed. Th. de Bruijn. *Frontiers of Indianness: Papers of the Leiden Seminar 2000.* New Delhi: Sahitya Akademi, (forthcoming).

—. "The Treatment of Women and Gender in the Plays *Āṣāṛh kā ek din* and *Ādhe adhūre* by Mohan Rākeś (1935 - 1972)." Ed. Dirk W. Loenne. *Toḥwa-e-dil: Festschrift Helmut Nespital.* Reinbek: Wezlar, 2001. 177-88.

—. *Gender, Religion and Modern Hindi Drama* (forthcoming).

—. *Upendranāth Aśk's Dramatic Work: Women and Gender in Modern Hindi Drama and as Revealed in the Plays of Upendranāth Aśk (1910-1996). University Dissertation.* Heidelberg: Microfiche Edition, 2000.

Freytag, Gustav. *Die Technik des Dramas.* Leipzig: Hirzel, 1894.

Gaeffke, P. "Der Zusammenbruch der Illusionen." *Hindiromane in der ersten Haelfte des 20. Jhd.s.* By P. Gaeffke. Leiden / Koeln, 1966. (chapter 5)

—. *Hindi Literature in the 20th Century: A History of Indian Literature.* Ed. Jan Gonda. Vol. VIII.5. Wiesbaden: Otto Harrassowitz, 1978. 55-61. 93-104.

Geiger, Heinz, and Hermann Haarmann. *Aspekte des Dramas.* Opladen: Westdeutscher Verlag, 1978.

Handa, R. L. *A History of Hindi Language and Literature.* Bombay: Bharatiya Vidya Bhavan, 1978. 369-387.

Hansen, Kathryn. *Grounds for Play: The Nauṭaṅkī Theatre of North India.* Berkeley: University of California Press, 1992.

Hawkes, Terence. *Structuralism and Semiotics.* London: Routledge, 1988.

Henig, Suzanne. "The Bloomsbury Group and Non-Western Literature." *Journal of South Asian Literature* 10 (1974-75): 73-82.

Jain, Nemicandra. *Indian Theatre: Tradition, Continuity and Change.* New Delhi: Vikas, 1992.

Jehlen, Myra. "Gender." *Critical Terms for Literary Study*. Ed. Frank Lentricchia and Thomas McLaughlin. Chicago: University of Chicago Press, 1990. 263-274.

Karnad, Girish. "Theatre in India." *Daedalus: Journal of the American Academy of Arts and Sciences* Fall 1989: 331-53.

Klotz, Volker. *Geschlossene und offene Form im Drama*. 1960. Muenchen: Hanser, 1992.

Lechte, John. *Fifty Key Contemporary Thinkers from Structuralism to Postmodernity*. London: Routledge, 1994.

Lukács, Georg. *Entwicklungsgeschichte des modernen Dramas: Georg Lukács Werke*. Ed. Frank Benseler. Vol. 15. Darmstadt and Neuwied: Luchterhand, 1981.

——. "Zur Soziologie des modernen Dramas." *Schriften zur Literatursoziologie*. By G. Lukács. Neuwied: Luchterhand, 1972. 261-295.

Manchi, Sarat Babu. *Indian Drama Today: A Study in the Theme of Cultural Deformity*. New Delhi: Prestige Books. 1997.

Meisig, Konrad. "Kālidāsa's Life and Works as Reflected in Mohan Rākeś's Play *Āṣāṛh kā ek din*." *Tender Ironies: A Tribute to Lothar Lutze*. Ed. Dilip Chitre et al. New Delhi: Manohar, 1994. 286-307.

Morris, Wesley. *Toward a New Historicism*. Princeton: Princeton University Press, 1972.

Paranjape, Makarand, ed. *Nativism: Essays in Criticism*. New Delhi: Sahitya Akademi, 1997.

Pettit, Philip. *The Concept of Structuralism: A Critical Analysis*. Berkeley: University of California Press, 1977.

Pfister, Manfred. *Das Drama: Theorie und Analyse*. rev. ed. Muenchen: Wilhelm Fink Verlag, 1988.

Potabenko, S. "K istorii razvitija sceničeskoj dramaturgii i teatra chindustani." *Literatury Indii: Sbornik statej*. ed. I. S. Rabinovič i E.P. Celyśev. Moskva: Izdatel'stvo vostočnoj literatury, 1958. 105-148.

——. *Dramaturgija chindi v bor'be za svobodu i nezavisimost' Indii*. Moskva: Izdatel'stvo vostočnoj literatury, 1962.

Rabinovič, S. "P'esa 'Puti raschodjatsja' kak važnejśij etap stanovlenija realizma v tvorčestve Upendranatha Aśka." *Dramaturgija i teatr Indii, sbornik statej*. Moskva: Izdatel'stvo vostočnoj literatury, 1961. 189-234.

Rimmon-Kenan, Shlomith. *Narrative Fiction: Contemporary Poetics.* London and New York: Methuen, 1983.

Robinson, Lillian. *Sex, Class and Culture.* New York: Methuen, 1986.

Rockwell, Anne Daisy. *The Novelty of Ashk: Conflict, Originality and Novelization in the Life and Work of Upendranath Ashk (1910–1996).* Diss. U. of Chicago, 1998. Ann Arbor: UMI, 1998. 9832167.

Schomer, Karine. *Mahadevi Varma and the Chayavad Age of Modern Hindi Poetry.* Berkeley: University of California Press, 1983. 124-50.

Shonek, Romesh K. "Upendranath Ashk: A Brief Biography and the Theme of Society and Self in His Semi-Autobiographical Trilogy." Allahabad: Neelabh, n.d.

Szondi, Peter. *Theorie des modernen Dramas.* 1956. Frankfurt/M: Suhrkamp 27, 1970.

Toolan, Michael J. *Narrative: A Critical Linguistic Introduction.* London and New York: Routledge, 1988.

Veeser, Harold. *The New Historicism.* New York: Routledge, Chapman & Hall, 1989.

Viśnevskaja, N. A. *Indijskaja odnooktnaja drama.* Moskva: Izdatel'stvo Nauka, 1964.

Watson, G. J. *Drama: An Introduction.* London and Basingstoke: Macmillan Press, 1983.

Zwecker, Karin. "Interpretation zwoelf ausgewaehlter Einakter von Upendranath Ashk." M.A. thesis, Johannes Gutenberg Universitaet zu Mainz, 1980.

Glossary

agar	-	but
āp	-	you (polite, honorific form)
aparājitā	-	unconquered
atyācār	-	tyranny
baṛī laṛkī	-	big girl
bhor kā tārā	-	morning star, transient, something that has momentary existence
choṭī laṛkī	-	little girl
dāsī(s)	-	female slave(s)
deśīvād	-	nativism
devanāgarī	-	the Devanagari syllabic alphabet
ekāṅkī	-	one-act play
gaṇ-mukhya	-	chief of a community
gṛhasvāmī	-	householder
gṛhasvāminī	-	householder's wife

goṣṭhī(s)	-	seminar(s)
indrajāl	-	magic
insān	-	human being
jīvan	-	life
jo	-	who, which
laṛkā	-	boy
lekin	-	but
magar	-	but
mahant	-	head priest of a temple
manuṣya	-	human being
māyā	-	illusion
moṭī ramṇī	-	fat young woman
nāṭak	-	drama
nāyak	-	hero
nāyikā	-	heroine
paṇḍit	-	Sanskrit scholar; learned person
pratibhā	-	genius, brilliance
puruṣ cār	-	man number four

puruṣ do	-	man number two
puruṣ ek	-	man number one
puruṣ tīn	-	man number three
rāj	-	kingdom
rānī	-	queen
sūtradhār	-	stage manager of a dramatic performance
strī	-	woman
ṭakā	-	a copper coin, worth half an *anna*
tilisma	-	magic
tum	-	you (informal form)
upakram	-	prelude
upsaṃhār	-	epilogue
ūsar	-	fallow, barren land
videśī	-	foreign
zindagī	-	life
zulm	-	tyranny

Dramas

Aśk, Upendranāth

Ādi mārg (The Primordial Way), 1943
Alag alag rāste (Separate Ways), 1954
Andhī galī (Blind Alley), 1956
Añjo Dīdī (The Elder Sister Añjo), 1955
Batsiyā (*Batsiya*), publication year 1971
Bhaṃvar (Whirlpool), 1961
Camatkār (Marvel), 1941
Carvāhe (The Herdsmen), 1942
Chaṭhā beṭā (The Sixth Son), 1950
Jay parājay (Victory and Defeat), 1937
Kaid aur Uṛān (Prison and Flight), 1950
Lakṣmī kā svāgat (Lakṣmī's Welcome), 1938
Nayā Purānā (New and Old), 1948
Pāpī (The Sinner), 1937-8
Pardā uṭhāo! Pardā girāo (Raise the Curtain! Drop the Curtain), 1951
Svarg kī jhalak (Glimpse of Paradise), 1939
Taulie (Towels), 1943
Tūfān se pahle (Before the Storm), 1946

Beckett, Samuel

En attendant Godot, 1953

Bhuvaneśvar (Bhuvaneśvar Prasād Śrīvāstav)

Lāṭrī (Lottery), 1935
Pratibhā kā vivāh (Pratibhā's Marriage), 1933
Romāns: Romāñc (Romance: Horripilation), 1935
Ūsar (Fallow Land), 1938

Hariścandra, Bhāratendu

Andher Nagarī (The Lawless State), 1881

Māthur, Jagdiścandra

Bhor kā Tārā (The Morning Star), 1937
Koṇārk (The Temple of Konark), 1951

Miller, Arthur

Death of a Salesman, 1949

Miśra, Lakṣmīnārāyāṇ

Sanyāsī (The Ascetic), 1929

Prasād, Jayśaṅkar

Candragupta (Candragupta), 1931

Rākeś, Mohan

Ādhe adhūre (Incomplete Halves), 1969

Strindberg, August

Play with Fire, 1892
Dance of Death, 1900
The Father, 1887
To Damascus, 1898–1904

Wilder, Thornton

Our Town, 1938
The Long Christmas Dinner, 1931

Author Index

Subject Index

Asian Thought and Culture

This series is designed to cover three inter-related projects:

- *Asian Classics Translation*, including those modern Asian works that have been generally accepted as "classics"
- *Asian and Comparative Philosophy and Religion*, including excellent and publishable Ph.D. dissertations, scholarly monographs, or collected essays
- *Asian Thought and Culture in a Broader Perspective*, covering exciting and publishable works in Asian culture, history, political and social thought, education, literature, music, fine arts, performing arts, martial arts, medicine, etc.

For additional information about this series or for the submission of manuscripts, please contact:

Peter Lang Publishing, Inc.
Acquisitions Department
275 Seventh Avenue, 28th floor
New York, New York 10001

To order other books in this series, please contact our Customer Service Department at:

800-770-LANG (within the U.S.)
(212) 647-7706 (outside the U.S.)
(212) 647-7707 FAX

Or browse online by series at:

www.peterlangusa.com